Logical Deduction Puzzles

George J. Summers

**Official Mensa
Puzzle Book**

Sterling Publishing Co., Inc.
New York

Mensa and the distinctive table logo are trademarks of
American Mensa, Ltd. (in the U.S.),
British Mensa, Ltd. (in the U.K.),
Australian Mensa, Inc. (in Australia),
and Mensa International Limited (in other countries)
and are used by permission.

Mensa as an organization does not express an opinion as being that of Mensa or
have any ideological, philosophical, political or religious affiliations. Mensa
specifically disclaims any responsibility for any liability, loss or risk, personal or
otherwise, which is incurred as a consequence, directly or indirectly, of the use
and application of any of the contents of this book.

Library of Congress Cataloging-in-Publication Data
Summers, George J.
  Logical deduction puzzles / George J. Summers.
     p. cm.
  Rev. ed. of: New puzzles in logical deduction. New York : Dover Publications,
1968.
  Includes index.
  ISBN-13: 978-1-4027-2133-5
  ISBN-10: 1-4027-2133-1
1. Logic puzzles. I. Summers, George J. New puzzles in logical deduction. II.
Title.

GV1493.S866 2006
793.73—dc22   2006002285

10 9 8 7 6 5 4

Published by Sterling Publishing Co., Inc.
387 Park Avenue South, New York, NY 10016
© 2006 by George J. Summers
Revised edition of *New Puzzles in Logical Deduction*
© 1968 by George J. Summers
Distributed in Canada by Sterling Publishing
c/o Canadian Manda Group, 165 Dufferin Street
Toronto, Ontario, Canada M6K 3H6
Distributed in the United Kingdom by GMC Distribution Services
Castle Place, 166 High Street, Lewes, East Sussex, England BN7 1XU
Distributed in Australia by Capricorn Link (Australia) Pty. Ltd.
P.O. Box 704, Windsor, NSW 2756, Australia

Manufactured in the United States of America
All rights reserved

Sterling ISBN-13: 978-1-4027-2133-5
       ISBN-10: 1-4027-2133-1

For information about custom editions, special sales, premium and corporate
purchases, please contact Sterling Special Sales Department at 800-805-5489 or
specialsales@sterlingpub.com.

Contents

Introduction

The puzzles in this book have been composed to resemble short who-dunit mysteries. Each puzzle contains a number of clues, and it is up to the reader—or "detective"—to determine from these clues which of various solutions is correct (or, to continue the analogy, which of various suspects is the culprit). In some of the puzzles an actual criminal must be sought, but the greater part of them concern more-or-less innocent people or things.

The general method for solving these puzzles is as follows: The question posed at the end of each puzzle states a condition that must be met by the solution. For example, "which one of the four teams—the Alleycats, the Bobcats, the Cougars, or the Domestics—won the pennant?" specifies "won the pennant" as a condition. The clues also specify conditions involving the various "suspects." What the "detective" must do is take into account all the conditions in order to discover which one—and only one—"suspect" satisfies the condition stated in the question.

Should you need help in deciding what you have to do in order to solve a particular puzzle, you can turn to the Solving Strategy provided for that puzzle to set you on the right path.

Of the puzzles in this book, most require no special knowledge. The rules of play for The Hostess, The Club Trick, and The Tenth Trick are based on the card game of bridge, but you do not need to know how to play bridge in order to solve these three puzzles.

Fourteen puzzles, however, call for some knowledge of simple high-school algebra. If such instruction has been lacking or that knowledge has become a bit rusty over the years, these puzzles can be considered a pleasurable introduction to algebra or a refresher course.

Puzzles

The Best Player

Mr. Scott, his sister, his son, and his <u>daughter</u> are tennis players. The following facts refer to the people mentioned:

1. The best player's twin and the worst player are of opposite sex.
2. The best player and the worst player are the same age.

Which one of the four is the best player?

Solving strategy, page 49 / Solution, page 71.

Mary's Ideal Man

Mary's ideal man is tall, dark, and handsome. She knows four men: Alec, Bill, Carl, and Dave.

1. Only three of the men are tall, only two are dark, and only one is handsome.
2. Each of the four men has at least one of the required traits.
3. Alec and Bill have the same complexion.
4. Bill and Carl are the same height.
5. Carl and Dave are not both tall.
6. One of the four men has all of the characteristics Mary requires.

Which one of the four men satisfies all of Mary's requirements?

Solving strategy, page 49 / Solution, page 71.

Middletown

Middletown includes the homes of four salesmen: Arden, Blair, Clyde, and Duane.

1. Each of the four homes is located at an intersection of two or more streets as indicated in the following map of the town:

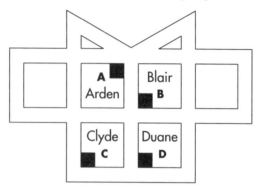

2. One day, Arden visited the home of his best friend Blair, Blair visited the home of his best friend Clyde, Clyde visited the home of his best friend Duane, and Duane visited the home of his best friend Arden.

3. On that day, each salesman's journey
   a. Began with his leaving his own home and ended with his arriving at his best friend's home;
   b. Involved stopping at some homes along each block in Middletown (a "block" is a part of a street that is between two intersections with homes on either one of two sides);
   c. Resulted in only one of the four men being able to travel along each block in Middletown exactly once.

Which one of the four men traveled along each block in Middletown exactly once?

Solving strategy, page 49 / Solution, page 72.

Murder in the Family

Murder occurred one evening in the home of a father and mother and their son and daughter. One member of the family murdered another member, the third member witnessed the crime, and the fourth member was an accessory after the fact.

F/S
1. The accessory and the witness were of opposite sex.
2. The oldest member and the witness were of opposite sex. M/D
3. The youngest member and the victim were of opposite sex.
4. The accessory was older than the victim. M/F
5. The father was the oldest member.
6. The murderer was not the youngest member.

M
F
D
S

Which one of the four—father, mother, son, or daughter—was the murderer?

Solving strategy, page 50 / Solution, page 73.

Three A's

In the multiplication problem below, each letter represents a different one of the ten digits: 0, 1, 2, 3, 4, 5, 6, 7, 8, 9.

$$
\begin{array}{r}
A\ S \\
\times\quad A \\
\hline
M\ A\ N
\end{array}
$$

Which one of the ten digits does A represent?

Solving strategy, page 50 / Solution, page 73.

Everybody Lied

When a psychiatrist was found murdered in his apartment, four of his patients were questioned about his death.

- I. The police knew from the testimony of witnesses that each of the four patients had been alone with the psychiatrist in his apartment just once on the day of his death.
- II. Before the four patients were questioned, they met and agreed that every statement each of them would make to the police would be a lie.

Each patient made two statements, as follows:

AVERY:　　1. None of us four killed the psychiatrist.
　　　　　　2. The psychiatrist was alive when I left.
BLAKE:　　3. I was the second to arrive.
　　　　　　4. The psychiatrist was dead when I arrived.
CROWN:　　5. I was the third to arrive.
　　　　　　6. The psychiatrist was alive when I left.
DAVIS:　　7. The killer did not arrive after I did.
　　　　　　8. The psychiatrist was dead when I arrived.

Which one of the four patients killed the psychiatrist?

Solving strategy, page 50 / Solution, page 74.

The Triangular Pen

A farmer built a trianglular pen for his chickens. The pen was made of a wire mesh attached to posts imbedded in the ground.

1. The wire mesh, of uniform width, was attached to the posts at equal heights above the ground.
2. The farmer made the following entry—costs are proportional to the amounts of wire mesh used—in a notebook:
      Cost of wire mesh for side of pen facing barn: $10
      Cost of wire mesh for side of pen facing pond: $20
      Cost of wire mesh for side of pen facing home: $30
3. He paid for the wire mesh with only ten-dollar bills, and received no change.
4. He paid with a different number of ten-dollar bills for the wire mesh along each side of the pen.
5. Exactly one of the three costs in his entry was incorrect.

Which one of the three costs was incorrect?

Solving strategy, page 51 / Solution, page 74.

Speaking of Bets

"The three of us made some bets," someone said.

1. "First, A won from B as much as A had originally.
2. Next, B won from C as much as B then had left.
3. Finally, C won from A as much as C then had left.
4. We ended up having equal amounts of money.
5. I began with 50 cents."

Which one of the three—A, B, or C—is the speaker?

Solving strategy, page 52 / Solution, page 75.

The Trump Suit

In a certain card game, one of the hands dealt contains:

1. Exactly thirteen cards.
2. At least one card in each of four suits—spades, hearts, diamonds, clubs.
3. A different number of cards in each suit.
4. A total of five hearts and diamonds.
5. A total of six hearts and spades.
6. Exactly two cards in the "trump" suit.

Which one of the four suits is the "trump" suit?

Solving strategy, page 52 / Solution, page 75.

Malice and Alice

Alice, Alice's husband, their son, their daughter, and Alice's brother were involved in a murder. One of the five killed one of the other four. The following facts refer to the five people mentioned:

1. A man and a woman were together in a bar at the time of the murder.
2. The victim and the killer were together on a beach at the time of the murder.
3. One of Alice's two children was alone at the time of the murder.
4. Alice and her husband were not together at the time of the murder.
5. The victim's twin was not the killer.
6. The killer was younger than the victim.

Which one of the five was the victim?

Solving strategy, page 52 / Solution, page 76.

A Week in Arlington

In the town of Arlington, the supermarket, the department store, and the bank are open together on one day each week.

1. Each of the three places is open four days a week.
2. On Sunday all three places are closed.
3. None of the three places is open on three consecutive days.
4. On six consecutive days:

    the department store was closed on the first day,

    the supermarket was closed on the second day,

    the bank was closed on the third day,

    the supermarket was closed on the fourth day,

    the department store was closed on the fifth day, and

    the bank was closed on the sixth day.

On which one of the seven days in a week are all three places in Arlington open?

Solving strategy, page 53 / Solution, page 77.

Eunice's Marital Status

At a party Jack saw Eunice standing alone at the punch bowl.

1. There were nineteen people altogether at the party.
2. Each of seven people came alone; each of the rest came with a member of the opposite sex.
3. The couples who came to the party were either engaged to each other or married to each other.
4. The women who came alone were unattached.
5. No man who came alone was engaged.
6. The number of engaged men present equaled the number of married men present.
7. The number of married men who came alone equaled the number of unattached men who came alone.
8. Of the married women, engaged women, and unattached women present, Eunice belonged to the largest group.
9. Jack, who was unattached, wanted to know which group of women Eunice belonged to.

Was Eunice married, engaged, or unattached?

Solving strategy, page 53 / Solution, page 78.

A Smart Man

Aaron, Brian, and Colin are studying Chemistry and Physics.

Aaron says truthfully:
1. Only one of us is smart.
2. If I am not smart, I will not pass Chemistry.

Brian says truthfully:
3. The smart man is the only man not to pass one of the two subjects.
4. If I am smart, I will pass Chemistry.

Colin says truthfully:
5. If I am smart, I will pass Physics.
6. If I am not smart, I will not pass Physics.

Which one of the three men is smart?

Solving strategy, page 54 / Solution, page 78.

The Murderer

Three suspects—Adam, Brad, and Cole—were questioned at different times about the murder of Dale.

1. Each man made a different one of the statements listed below referring to another of the suspects.
    Statement X. Adam is innocent of the murder.
    Statement Y. Brad is telling the truth.
    Statement Z. Cole is lying.
2. Statement X was made first; but Statements Y and Z are not necessarily in chronological order, though each refers to a statement made earlier.
3. The murderer, who was one of the three men, made a false statement.

Which one of the three men was the murderer?

Solving strategy, page 54 / Solution, page 79.

The Missing Digit

In the addition problem below, each letter represents a different digit:

$$
\begin{array}{r}
A\ B \\
C\ D \\
E\ F \\
+\ G\ H \\
\hline
I\ \ I\ \ I
\end{array}
$$

Which one of the ten digits—0, 1, 2, 3, 4, 5, 6, 7, 8, 9—is missing?

Solving strategy, page 54 / Solution, page 80.

One, Two, or Four

A coin game requires:

1. Ten coins in one pile.
2. That each player take one, two, or four coins from the pile at alternate turns.
3. That the player who takes the last coin loses.

   I. When Austin and Brooks play, Austin goes first and Brooks goes second.
  II. Each player always makes a move that allows him to win when possible; if there is no way for him to win, then he always makes a move that allows a tie when possible.

Must one of the two men win? If so, which one?

Solving strategy, page 55 / Solution, pages 81–82.

Hubert's First Watch

Hubert was one of a group of men hired by a jewelry company as an early-morning watchman.

1. For no more than 100 days Hubert was on a rotating system of standing watch.
2. Hubert's first and last watches were the only ones of his to occur on a Sunday.
3. Hubert's first and last watches occurred on the same date of different months.
4. The months in which Hubert's first and last watches occurred had the same number of days.

In which one of the twelve months did Hubert have his first watch?

Solving strategy, page 55 / Solution, pages 83–84.

The Student Thief

Professor Winter's answer key to a Biology test was stolen during one of his Biology classes. Only three students—Amos, Burt, and Cobb—had the opportunity to steal the answer key.

1. Five Biology classes had been held in the lab that week.
2. Amos attended only two of the classes.
3. Burt attended only three of the classes.
4. Cobb attended only four of the classes.
5. The professor conducted only three of the classes.
6. Each of the three students attended only two of the professor's classes.
7. No two of the five classes were attended by the same group of students from the three students under suspicion.
8. Two of the three students, who attended one of the professor's classes that the third student did not attend, were proven innocent of the theft.

Which one of the three students stole the answer key?

Solving strategy, page 56 / Solution, pages 84–85.

The Four Groves

Mr. Sloan has four groves: an apple grove, a lemon grove, an orange grove, and a peach grove.

1. Each grove consists of trees that are uniformly spaced out like this

<pre>
O O O O O O ...
O O O O O O ...
O O O O O O ...
: : : : : :
</pre>

   with an indeterminate but same number of trees in each row going from west to east and similarly the same number of trees in each row going from north to south.

2. Counting the rows of trees going from north to south: the apple grove has the least number, the lemon grove has one more number than the apple grove, the orange grove has one more number than the lemon grove, and the peach grove has one more number than the orange grove.

3. The number of trees in the interior of each of three groves equals the number of trees on its border.

In which one of the four groves does the number of trees in the interior not equal the number of trees on its border?

Solving strategy, page 56 / Solution, pages 85–86.

The Square Table, Part I

Alden, Brent, Clark, and Doyle were seated around a square table in a restaurant when Doyle fell dead from poison. When questioned by a detective each man made two statements as follows:

ALDEN: 1. I sat next to Brent.
         2. Brent or Clark sat on my right, and the person on my right could not have poisoned Doyle.

BRENT: 3. I sat next to Clark.
         4. Alden or Clark sat on Doyle's right, and the person on Doyle's right could not have poisoned Doyle.

CLARK: 5. I sat across from Doyle.
         6. The poisoner is making at least one false statement.

After talking to the waiter who had served them, the detective told them truthfully:

         7. Only one of you lied at least once.
         8. One of you poisoned Doyle.

Which one of the three men poisoned Doyle?

Solving strategy, page 57 / Solution, pages 86–87.

The Square Table, Part II

The wives of Alden, Brent, and Clark witnessed Doyle's death by poison when the four men were seated around the square table in the restaurant. When questioned by the detective, each woman made two statements, referring to the suspects by their first names, as follows:

RAY'S WIFE:
1. Ray sat next to Sid.
2. Sid or Ted sat on Ray's right, and the person on Ray's right could not have poisoned Doyle.

SID'S WIFE:
3. Sid sat next to Ted.
4. Ray or Ted sat on Doyle's right, and the person on Doyle's right could not have poisoned Doyle.

TED'S WIFE:
5. Ted sat next to Doyle.
6. The poisoner's wife is making at least one false statement.

After talking to the waiter who had served the four men, the detective told the women truthfully:

7. Only one of you lied at least once.

Which one of the three women was the poisoner's wife?

NOTE: *The solution to Part II must be consistent with the statements in Part I.*

Solving strategy, page 57 / Solution, pages 87–88.

The Two Brothers

Albert, Barney, Curtis, Dwight, Emmett, and Farley are art collectors, two of whom are brothers. One day, when they were all at an art fair, the men bought art objects as described below:

1. The price of each art object was a whole number of cents.
2. Albert bought 1 art object, Barney bought 2, Curtis bought 3, Dwight bought 4, Emmett bought 5, and Farley bought 6.
3. The two brothers paid the same amount for each of the art objects they bought.
4. Each of the other four men paid twice as much for each art object they bought as the two brothers paid for each of their art objects.
5. Altogether the six men spent $1,000 for the art objects they bought.

Which two of the six men are brothers?

Solving strategy, page 57 / Solution, pages 88–89.

One, Three, or Four

A coin game requires:

1. Nine coins in one pile.
2. That each player take one, three, or four coins from the pile at alternate turns.
3. That the player who takes the last coin wins.

  I. When Audrey and Bonita play, Audrey goes first and Bonita goes second.
  II. Each player always makes a move that allows her to win, if possible; if there is no way for her to win, then she always makes a move that allows a tie, if possible.

Must one of the two women win? If so, which one?

Solving strategy, page 57 / Solution, pages 90–91.

A Timely Death

One evening four explorers named Xavier, Yeoman, Zenger, and Osborn made separate camps along the banks of a river.

Wilson, a fifth explorer camped in the country's interior, communicated with the other men by radio at various times during the night. When he received no reply from Osborn after 10:30 that night, Wilson communicated with the other three men to express his concern.

The next morning Osborn was found dead; he had been murdered. Evidence at the scene of the crime indicated that the killer had approached Osborn's camp by boat from the river. Xavier, Yeoman, and Zenger had each had access to a canoe on the previous night.

Wilson suspected that either Xavier, Yeoman, or Zenger had killed Osborn. From the following facts, Wilson was able to eliminate two of these men as suspects.

1. Osborn was killed in his camp before 10:30 on the previous night; he had been shot and had died instantly.
2. The killer traveled to Osborn's camp and returned to his own camp by canoe.
3. Xavier's camp was located directly downstream from Osborn's camp, Yeoman's camp was located directly across the river from Osborn's camp, and Zenger's camp was located directly upstream from Osborn's camp.
4. At least 80 minutes were needed for each of the three men to make the round trip to and from Osborn's camp by canoe.
5. There was a strong current in the river.
6. Wilson received replies to his radio calls at the following times:

    From Osborn at 9:15

    From Xavier at 8:15, 9:40, and 10:55

    From Yeoman at 8:20, 9:45, and 11:00

    From Zenger at 8:25, 9:50, and 11:05

Which one of the three men could Wilson not eliminate as a suspect?

Solving strategy, page 58 / Solution, pages 91–92.

Turnabout

PROBLEM I	PROBLEM II	PROBLEM III
A R B	A R S B	A R S T B
× C	× C	× C

1. In each of the three multiplication problems above, each letter represents a different digit; however, each letter does not necessarily represent the same digit in one problem as it does in another problem.
2. In each of two of these multiplication problems, the digits in the product are the same as the digits in the number multiplied by C, except that the order is reversed.

In which one of the three multiplication problems are the digits in the product not the same as the digits in the number multiplied by C?

Solving strategy, page 58 / Solution, pages 92–94.

A Week in Burmingham

The town of Burmingham has a supermarket, a department store, and a bank. On the day I went into Burmingham, the bank was open.

1. The supermarket, the department store, and the bank are not open together on any day of the week.
2. The department store is open four days a week.
3. The supermarket is open five days a week.
4. All three places are closed on Sunday and Wednesday.
5. On three consecutive days:
   the bank was closed on the first day,
   the supermarket was closed on the second day, and
   the department store was closed on the third day.
6. On three consecutive days:
   the department store was closed on the first day,
   the bank was closed on the second day, and
   the supermarket was closed on the third day.

On which one of the seven days in a week did I go into the town of Burmingham?

Solving strategy, page 59 / Solution, pages 94–95.

Cards on the Table

Eight numbered cards lie facedown on a table in the relative positions shown in the diagram below.

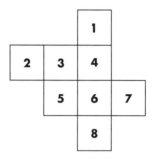

With reference to the rows and columns, of the eight cards:

1. There is at least one Queen between two Kings.
2. There is at least one King between two Jacks.
3. No Jack borders on a Queen.
4. There is exactly one Ace.
5. No King borders on the Ace.
6. At least one King borders on a King.
7. Each card is either a King, a Queen, a Jack, or an Ace.

Which one of the eight numbered cards is the Ace?

Solving strategy, page 59 / Solution, page 95.

The Murderess

Three women—Anna, Babs, and Cora—were questioned about the murder of Dana. One of the three women committed the murder, the second was an accomplice in the murder, and the third was innocent of any involvement in the murder.

1. Each of the following three statements was made by one of the three women, referring to another of the women.
    Statement X: Anna is not the accomplice.
    Statement Y: Babs is not the murderess.
    Statement Z: Cora is not the innocent one.
2. The innocent woman made at least one of these statements.
3. Only the innocent woman told the truth.

Which one of the three women was the murderess?

Solving strategy, page 59 / Solution, page 96.

Conversation Stopper

Amelia, Brenda, Cheryl, and Denise went to a party.

1. By 8 P.M., Amelia and her husband having already arrived at the party, there were no more than 100 people, all conversing in groups of five people each.
2. By 9 P.M., only Brenda and her husband having arrived at the party after 8 P.M., the people were conversing in groups of four people each.
3. By 10 P.M., only Cheryl and her husband having arrived at the party after 9 P.M., the people were conversing in groups of three people each.
4. By 11 P.M., only Denise and her husband having arrived after 10 P.M., the people were conversing in groups of two people each.
5. One of the four women mentioned, who suspected her husband of infidelity, had planned to let her husband go to the party without her, and then to arrive at the party one hour later, but she changed her mind.
6. If the woman who suspected her husband of infidelity had carried out her plan, it would have been impossible for the people—including her husband but not herself—to converse in smaller groups containing equal numbers of people at one of the four times mentioned.

Which one of the four women suspected her husband of infidelity?

Solving strategy, pages 59–60 / Solution, pages 97–98.

The Constant Winner

Abe, Ben, Cal, and Don played some games in which they took turns drawing chips from a pile. The same man won every game.

1. The four men played 10 games with an even number of chips in a pile at the beginning of each game: eight chips in a pile at the beginning of the first game, ten chips in a pile at the beginning of the second game, and so on through 26 chips in a pile at the beginning of the tenth game.
2. During the entire series of 10 games, each of the four men always took the same number of chips: he always took one chip or he always took two chips; if only one chip remained and a player had decided to always take two chips, he "passed" and the turn went to the next player.
3. The order in which they took chips from a pile was always the same: first Abe, then Ben, then Cal, then Don.
4. The player who took the last chip was the winner in each game.

Which one of the four men won every game?

Solving strategy, page 60 / Solution, page 98.

The Woman Hector Will Marry

Hector has been dating three women: Annette, Bernice, and Claudia.

Annette says truthfully:
1. If I talk a lot, then Bernice talks a lot.
2. If I am stubborn, then Claudia is stubborn.

Bernice says truthfully:
3. If I nag, then Claudia nags.
4. If I talk a lot, then Annette talks a lot.

Claudia says truthfully:
5. If I nag, then Annette nags.
6. If Bernice is stubborn, then I am not stubborn.

Hector says truthfully:
7. Each of the three traits—talks a lot, nags, is stubborn—is possessed by at least one of the three women.
8. Two of the women possess the same number and kind of unfortunate traits.
9. The woman I will marry is the only woman with exactly one unfortunate trait.

Which one of the three women will Hector marry?

Solving strategy, page 60 / Solution, page 99.

Father and Son

Arnold, Burton, Claude, and Dennis are stock brokers, one man of whom is the father of one of the other three men. One day when they were all at the stock exchange, the men bought shares as described below:

1. Arnold bought only shares at $3 each, Barton bought only shares at $4 each, Claude bought only shares at $6 each, and Dennis bought only shares at $8 each.
2. The father bought the greatest number of shares, paying $72 altogether.
3. The son bought the least number of shares, paying $24 altogether.
4. The total money spent by the four men for their combined shares was $161.

Which one of the four men is the father? Which one of the four men is his son?

Solving strategy, page 61 / Solution, pages 99–100.

The Race

Alan, Bart, Clay, and Dick competed in a race where each man finished in a different position. The four men, notorious liars, reported the results of the race as follows:

ALAN: 1. I came in immediately before Bart.
        2. I did not come in first.
BART: 3. I came in immediately before Clay.
        4. I did not come in second.
CLAY: 5. I came in immediately before Dick.
        6. I did not come in third.
DICK: 7. I came in immediately before Alan.
        8. I did not come in last.

    I. Only two of the above men's statements were true.
   II. The man who won the race made at least one true statement.

Which one of the four men won the race?

Solving strategy, page 60 / Solution, pages 100–101.

Murder by Profession

Bell and Cass were Alex White's sisters; Dean and Earl were Faye Black's brothers. (Alex is a man and Faye is a woman.) Their occupations were as listed below:

	Alex – doctor		Dean – doctor
Whites	Bell – doctor	Blacks	Earl – lawyer
	Cass – lawyer		Faye – lawyer

One night while two of these people were at a party, two were in a park, and two were at a movie, one of the two people in the park killed the other.

The following facts refer to the people mentioned above:

1. A doctor and a lawyer were at a party.
2. The two people at the movie had the same occupation.
3. The victim and the killer were twins.
4. The two people at the party were the killer's spouse and the victim's spouse.
5. The victim and the victim's spouse had different occupations.
6a. One of the two persons at the movie was the former spouse of one of the two persons at the party.
6b. The other person at the movie and the doctor at the party were former roommates (same sex).

NOTE: *"Spouse" refers to a person of the opposite sex.*

Which one of the six was the killer?

Solving strategy, page 62 / Solution, pages 101–102.

Six G's

In the multiplication problem below, each letter represents a different digit:

$$
\begin{array}{r}
A\ B\ C\ D\ E \\
\times\qquad\qquad F \\
\hline
G\ G\ G\ G\ G\ G
\end{array}
$$

Which one of the ten digits—0, 1, 2, 3, 4, 5, 6, 7, 8, 9—does G represent?

Solving strategy, page 63 / Solution, pages 102–103.

Two or Three

A coin game requires:

1. Twelve coins in one pile.
2. That each player take two or three coins from the pile at alternate turns.
3. That the player who takes the last coin loses.

I. When Armand and Buford play, Armand goes first and Buford goes second.
II. Each player always makes a move that allows him to win, if possible; if there is no way for him to win, then he always makes a move that allows a tie, if possible.

Must one of the two men win? If so, which one?

Solving strategy, pages 63–64 / Solution, pages 103–104.

A Week in Cantonville

In the town of Cantonville, the supermarket, the department store, and the bank are open together on only one day each week.

1. The supermarket is open five days a week.
2. The department store is open four days a week.
3. The bank is open three days a week.
4. On three consecutive days:
   the bank was closed on the first day,
   the department store was closed on the second day, and
   the supermarket was closed on the third day.
5. On Sunday all three places are closed.
6. The bank is not open on two consecutive days.
7. The department store is not open on three consecutive days.
8. The supermarket is not open on four consecutive days.
9. Neither Saturday nor Monday is the day on which all three places are open.

On which one of the seven days in a week are all three places in Cantonville open?

Solving strategy, page 64 / Solution, page 105.

The Bookshelf

When Mrs. Drake, the head librarian, asked each of her three assistants how many books would fill a certain bookshelf, she received the following replies:

MRS. ASTOR — "2 catalogs, 3 dictionaries, and 3 encyclopedias will exactly fill this shelf."

MRS. BRICE — "4 catalogs, 3 dictionaries, and 2 encyclopedias will exactly fill this shelf."

MRS. CRANE — "4 catalogs, 4 dictionaries, and 3 encyclopedias will exactly fill this shelf."

1. Only two of the assistants were correct in their replies.
2. Attempting to fill the shelf with books of the same type, Mrs. Drake discovered that only one type—catalog, dictionary, or encyclopedia—would exactly fill the shelf.
3. Mrs. Drake required 15 books of this one type to exactly fill the shelf.
4. All the catalogs were the same size, all the dictionaries were the same size, and all the encyclopedias were the same size.

Assuming that the books were of such widths as to make negligible the widths of the spaces between pairs of books, with which one of the three types of books did Mrs. Drake exactly fill the shelf?

Solving strategy, pages 64–65 / Solution, pages 106–107.

The Hostess

Four women were playing a card game in which each card has a numerical ranking and is one of four suits called *clubs*, *diamonds*, *hearts*, and *spades*. The play of four cards, one from each player's holding, is called a *trick*, and the suit of the card played first in a trick is referred to as the *suit led*.

In this card game (a) a player must *follow suit* (play a card in the suit led), if possible, at each trick (otherwise, a player may play any card); (b) a player who wins a trick must lead at the next trick. Ten tricks had already been played and there were three more tricks left to be played.

1. At trick number eleven: Alma led a club; Bess played a diamond, Cleo played a heart, and Dina played a spade—not necessarily in that order.
2. The hostess won the twelfth trick and led a heart at trick number thirteen.
3. A different person led at each of the last three tricks.
4. All four suits were played at each of the last three tricks, a *trump* winning each trick. (A trump is any card in a certain suit that may be (a) played when a player has no cards in the suit led—in this event a card in the trump suit beats all cards in the other three suits; or (b) led, as any other suit may be led.)
5. A different person won each of the last three tricks.
6. The partner of the hostess held three red cards (either diamonds or hearts—clubs and spades are black cards).

Which one of the four women was the hostess?

Solving strategy, page 65 / Solution, pages 107–108.

The Rectangular Table

Harry and his wife Harriet gave a dinner party to which they invited: his brother Barry and Barry's wife Barbara; his sister Samantha and Samantha's husband Samuel; and his neighbor Nathan and Nathan's wife Natalie. While they were all seated at the table, one person produced a gun and shot another person. The chairs were arranged around the table as in the diagram below:

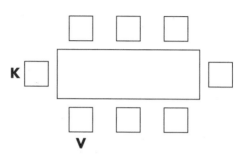

1. The killer sat in the chair marked K.
2. The victim sat in the chair marked V.
3. Every man sat opposite his wife.
4. The host was the only man who sat between two women (i.e., next to a woman on his left and next to a woman on his right), around the perimeter of the table).
5. The host did not sit next to his sister.
6. The hostess did not sit next to the host's brother.
7. The victim was the killer's former spouse (opposite sex).

Which one of the eight people was the killer?

Solving strategy, page 65 / Solution, pages 108–109.

Deanna's Sister

Deanna went shopping with her mother to buy some candy and small gifts for her sister's birthday party. Deanna's mother was going to buy the gifts, while Deanna was going to buy the candy. The number of candies bought and the number of gifts bought, together with the amount of money spent, are described below:

1. Deanna had with her thirteen coins, consisting of only three denominations—pennies, nickels, and quarters; she spent them all on the candy.
2. The candy she bought for Althea cost 2¢ each, the candy she bought for Blythe cost 3¢ each, and the candy she bought for Carrie cost 6¢ each.
3. She bought a different number of candies for each of the three girls, and she bought more than one candy for each girl.
4. For two kinds of candy she spent equal amounts of money.
5. Her mother bought a number of small gifts, each gift selling individually for the same amount of money; she paid $4.80 for the gifts.
6. The number of gifts bought was equal to the number of candies bought.
7. The girl for whom Deanna bought the greatest number of candies was her sister.

Which one of the three girls was Deanna's sister?

Solving strategy, pages 65–66 / Solution, pages 109–110.

The Cube

Three views of the same cube are shown below:

 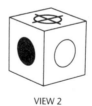 

VIEW 1　　　　　　　VIEW 2　　　　　　　VIEW 3

As can be seen, there is one of five different figures on each face shown in these views:

A little analysis indicates that one of these five figures must occur twice on the cube. In fact, any one of three figures can occur twice.

However, the owner of the cube states truthfully: "In each of the three views the figure that occurs twice is not on the bottom face of the cube." Now, only one figure can occur twice.

Which one of the five figures occurs twice on the cube?

NOTE: *If you find it difficult to visualize the cube's six faces, you might make a cube out of paper or draw a multiview cube as shown below. The bottom face will be the only face not seen.*

Solving strategy, page 66 / Solution, pages 111–112.

The Club Trick

Four women were playing a card game in which each card has a numeri-cal ranking and is one of four suits called *clubs*, *diamonds*, *hearts*, and *spades*. The play of four cards, one from each player's holding, is called a *trick* and the suit of the card played first in a trick is referred to as the *suit led*.

In this card game (a) a player must *follow suit* (play a card in the suit led), if possible, at each trick (otherwise, a player may play any card); (b) a player who wins a trick must lead at the next trick. Nine tricks had already been played and there were four more tricks left to be played.

1. The distribution of suits in the four hands was as follows:
   ADA'S HAND: club - heart - diamond - spade
   BEA'S HAND: club - heart - heart - diamond
   CYD'S HAND: club - heart - diamond - diamond
   DEB'S HAND: club - spade - spade - spade
2. Everyone played the same suit when one player led a club.
3. At exactly two tricks only one player followed suit.
4. A diamond was led at trick number ten.
5. A different person led at each of the last four tricks.
6. A different person won at each of the last four tricks.
7. A different suit was led at each of the last four tricks.
8. The highest card of the suit led won each trick.

Which one of the four women led the club?

Solving strategy, page 66 / Solution, pages 112–114.

Twelve C's

In the multiplication problem below, each letter represents a different digit:

```
        A B C D E F G H
      ×             A J
      ─────────────────
      E J A H F D G K C
      B D F H A J E C
      ─────────────────
      C C C C C C C C C
```

Which one of the ten digits—0, 1, 2, 3, 4, 5, 6, 7, 8, 9—does C represent?

Solving strategy, page 67 / Solution, pages 114–115.

John's Ideal Woman

John's ideal woman is blonde, blue-eyed, slender, and tall. He knows four women: Adele, Betty, Carol, and Doris. Only one of the four women has all four characteristics that John requires.

1. Only three of the women are both blue-eyed and slender.
2. Only two of the women are both blonde and tall.
3. Only two of the women are both slender and tall.
4. Only one of the women is both blue-eyed and blonde.
5. Adele and Betty have the same color eyes.
6. Betty and Carol have the same color hair.
7. Carol and Doris are not both slender.
8. Doris and Adele are the same height.

Which one of the four women satisfies all of John's requirements?

Solving strategy, page 67 / Solution, pages 116–117.

The L-Shaped Table

Abel and his wife Babe gave a party to which they invited four married couples. The four husbands invited were: Cain, Ezra, Gene, and Ivan. The four wives invited were: Dido, Fifi, Hera, and Joan.

While they were all seated at the table, one person stood up, produced a gun, and killed another person. The chairs were arranged around the oddly shaped table as shown in the diagram below:

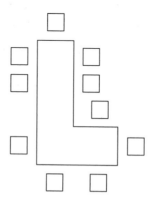

1. The people sat in alphabetical order going around the table counterclockwise.
2. The killer and the victim sat across the table from one another in the two newest chairs.
3. The killer's spouse and the victim's spouse sat across the table from one another in the two oldest chairs.
4. The only married couple to sit next to each other were the host and the hostess.
5. The victim did not sit next to the killer's spouse.
6. The host sat alone at one side of the (six-sided) table.
7. The killer did not sit alone at one side of the (six-sided) table.
8. Both the killer and the victim were guests.

Which one of the ten people was the killer?

Solving strategy, page 67 / Solution, pages 117–118.

The Tenth Trick

Four men were playing a card game in which each card has a numerical ranking and is one of four suits called *clubs, diamonds, hearts,* and *spades.* The play of four cards, one from each player's holding, is called a *trick* and the suit of the card played first in a trick is referred to as the *suit led.*

In this card game (a) a player must *follow suit* (play a card in the suit led), if possible, at each trick (otherwise, a player may play any card); (b) a player who wins a trick must lead at the next trick. Nine tricks had already been played and there were four more tricks left to be played.

1. The distribution of suits in the four hands was as follows:
    HAND I: club - diamond - spade - spade
    HAND II: club - diamond - heart - heart
    HAND III: club - heart - diamond - diamond
    HAND IV: club - heart - spade - spade
2. Art led a diamond at one trick.
3. Bob led a heart at one trick.
4. Cab led a club at one trick.
5. Dan led a spade at one trick.
6. A *trump* won each trick. (A trump is any card in a certain suit that may be (a) played when a player has no cards in the suit led—in this event a card in the trump suit beats all cards in the other three suits; or (b) led, as any other suit may be led.)
7. Art and Cab, who were partners, won two tricks; Bob and Dan, who were partners, won two tricks.

Which one of the four men won the tenth trick?

Solving strategy, page 68 / Solution, pages 118–119.

Robert's Position

Robert, Steven, and Thomas entered some track-and-field events.

1. In each event, three points, two points, and one point was awarded for first, second, and third position, respectively.
2. Duplicate points were given to those men who tied in any of these three positions.
3a. The total number of points scored by each of the three men in the pole vault, long jump, and high jump was the same as that scored by each of the other two men.
3b. This number of points was the same as the total number of points scored by the three men in each of these events.
4. Robert and Thomas tied for either first, second, or third position in the long jump.
5. Robert and Steven tied for either first, second, or third position in the high jump.
6. Steven scored no points in one of the three events and Thomas scored no points in one of the three events; otherwise, points were scored.

In which one of the three positions—first, second, or third—did Robert finish in the pole vault?

Solving strategy, page 68 / Solution, pages 119–121.

The Baseball Pennant

It was the last week of the baseball season, and in the Felidae League the Alleycats, the Bobcats, the Cougars, and the Domestics were all tied for first place. It was decided that there would be a series of play-off games in which each team would play one game with each of the other three teams; the team winning the most play-off games would win the pennant.

1. The distribution of runs scored by each team during the play-off games was as follows (listed alphabetically according to the teams' home cities):

	RUNS SCORED IN EACH OF THREE GAMES
Sexton-City Team	1 - 3 - 7
Treble-City Team	1 - 4 - 6
Ulster-City Team	2 - 3 - 6
Verdue-City Team	2 - 4 - 5

2. Each team won a different number of play-off games.
3. The score for each play-off game was different from that of any other play-off game.
4. The greatest difference in runs scored by two teams at any one game was 3 runs; this difference occurred only once when the team that lost the greatest number of play-off games lost by 3 runs.
5. Two teams scored the same number of runs during the first round and two teams scored the same number of runs during the second round of the play-off games. (A *round* consists of all the teams playing games simultaneously.)
6. During the last round the Alleycats scored the larger odd number of runs, the Bobcats scored the smaller odd number of runs, the Cougars scored the larger even number of runs, and the Domestics scored the smaller even number of runs.

Which one of the four teams—the Alleycats, the Bobcats, the Cougars, or the Domestics—won the pennant?

Solving strategy, page 69 / Solution, pages 121–122.

No Cause for Celebration

The Smiths, the Joneses, and the Browns have the habit of referring to their children by number, according to the order in which their children were born. The following statements refer to their children in this manner:

1. The second child born to each family has three brothers.
2. The third child born to each family has two sisters.
3. The fourth child born to the Joneses and the fourth child born to the Smiths have the same number of brothers.
4. The fifth child born to the Smiths and the fifth child born to the Browns have the same number of sisters.
5. The sixth child born to the Browns has the same number of brothers as the sixth child born to the Joneses has sisters.
6. Each family has a different number of children.
7. In only one family is the first-born a boy.
8. In only one family is the last-born a girl.
9. On the day that a first-born boy married a last-born girl, only two families had cause for celebration—the bride's and the groom's.

Which one of the three families had no cause for celebration that day?

Solving strategy, pages 69–70 / Solution, pages 123–125.

Solving Strategies

The Best Player

Uniquely match three of MR. SCOTT, HIS SISTER, HIS SON, and HIS DAUGHTER with BEST PLAYER, WORST PLAYER, and BEST PLAYER'S TWIN so that no condition is contradicted.

Mary's Ideal Man

Make a chart for yourself as follows:

	TALL?	DARK?	HANDSOME?
Is Alec			
Is Bill			
Is Carl			
Is Dave			

Write "yes" or "no" in each box so that no condition is contradicted.

Middletown

Make a chart for yourself as follows:

	LEAVE HIS INTERSECTION ONE MORE TIME THAN HE ENTERS IT?	ENTER HIS BEST FRIEND'S INTERSECTION ONE MORE TIME THAN HE LEAVES IT?	MAKE THE SPECIFIED JOURNEY?
Can Arden			
Can Blair			
Can Clyde			
Can Duane			

Write "yes" or "no" in each box so that no condition is contradicted.

Murder in the Family

First determine the sex of each of the murderer, accessory, victim, and witness; then uniquely match each member of the family with one of the four parts that each played in the murder.

Three A's

Show that A cannot equal each one of nine digits, so that it must equal the only one that remains.

Everybody Lied

Make a chart for yourself as follows:

	WAS PSYCHIATRIST ALIVE AT HIS ARRIVAL?	WAS PSYCHIATRIST ALIVE AT HIS DEPARTURE?	IN WHAT PLACE IN THE ORDER DID HE ARRIVE?
Avery			
Blake			
Crown			
Davis			

First write "yes," "no," or "don't know" in each box in the left and middle columns and then write "first," "second," "third," or "fourth" in each box in the right column so that no condition is contradicted.

The Triangular Pen

Make a chart for yourself as follows:

	POSSIBLE NUMBER OF TEN-DOLLAR BILLS FOR SIDE OF PEN FACING		
	BARN IS	POND IS	HOME IS
When possible numbers of ten-dollar bills for sides of pen facing barn and pond are correct,			
When possible numbers of ten-dollar bills for sides of pen facing barn and home are correct,			
When possible numbers of ten-dollar bills for sides of pen facing pond and home are correct,			

Write the number of possible ten-dollar bills in each box—"0" may be a number—so that no condition is contradicted.

Speaking of Bets

Make a chart for yourself as follows:

	A HAD HOW MANY CENTS?	**B** HAD HOW MANY CENTS?	**C** HAD HOW MANY CENTS?
At the beginning, in terms of a, b, or c,	a	b	c
After the first bet, in terms of a, b, and/or c			
After the next bet, in terms of a, b, and/or c,			
After the final bet, in terms of a, b, and/or c,			
At the beginning, in terms of a,	a		
At the beginning, in terms of cents,			

Complete the table by writing an expression in each box so that no condition is contradicted.

The Trump Suit

Determine the number of cards in each suit so that no condition is contradicted.

Malice and Alice

First find the locations of two pairs of people at the time of the murder and then determine who the killer and the victim were so that no condition is contradicted.

A Week in Arlington

Using "C" for closed and "O" for open, make a chart for yourself as follows:

	1ST	2ND	3RD	4TH	5TH	6TH	7TH
Department Store	C				C		O
Supermarket		C		C			O
Bank			C			C	O

Complete the chart, in order to first locate where Sunday is and then to find out which day of the week is the 7th day, so that no condition is contradicted.

Eunice's Marital Status

Make a chart for yourself as follows:

Let the

    *Number of married women = a

In terms of *a*, the

    Number of married men with wives = _____

    *Number of engaged women = _____

    Number of engaged men = _____

    Number of married men = _____

    Number of married men who came alone = _____

    Number of unattached men who came alone = _____

    *Number of unattached women = _____

The value of *a* = _____

So the

    *Number of married women = _____

    *Number of engaged women = _____

    *Number of unattached women = _____

Fill in each blank so that no condition is contradicted.

A Smart Man

Make a chart for yourself as follows:

	DOES ASSUMING X IS SMART LEAD TO A CONTRADICTION?	IF SO, WHICH CONDITION IS CONTRADICTED?
If X is Aaron,		
If X is Brian,		
If X is Colin,		

Write "yes" in two boxes and "no" in one box in the first column and write the number of a condition in two of the boxes in the second column.

The Murderer

Make a chart for yourself as follows:

	COULD STATEMENT HAVE BEEN MADE BY			
	ADAM?	BRAD?	COLE?	MURDERER?
Adam/innocent				
Brad/truth				
Cole/lying				

Write "yes" or "no" in each box so that no condition is contradicted.

The Missing Digit

Make a table for yourself as follows:

Sum of digits 0 through 9 = _____

Maximum number that can be carried to left column = _____

The letter I = _____

Sum of digits represented by A through I = _____

Missing digit = _____

Write a number in each blank so that each letter represents a different digit.

One, Two, or Four

Begin two tables for yourself as follows:

FROM A LOSING POSITION OF	IF A PLAYER DRAWS	HE LEAVES A WINNING POSITION OF
1	1	0

FROM A WINNING POSITION OF	DRAW (1, 2, OR 4)	TO LEAVE A LOSING POSITION OF
2	1	1

Complete each table—going up to 10 to determine whether 10 is a winning or a losing position—so that no condition is contradicted.

The Student Thief

Make a table for yourself as follows:

CLASS CONDUCTED BY	CLASSES ATTENDED BY		
	AMOS	BURT	COBB
Professor			
Professor			
Professor			
Another			
Another			

Place two Xs in the column for Amos, three Xs in the column for Burt, and four Xs in the column for Cobb—each X to represent attendance at a class conducted either by Professor Winter or by some other professor—so that no condition is contradicted.

The Four Groves

Make a chart for yourself as follows:

Number of trees along each of two opposite sides of three groves = x

Number of trees along each of the other two opposite sides = y

Number of trees on the border (in terms of x and y) = _____

Number of trees in the interior (in terms of x and y) = _____

x (in terms of y) or y (in terms of x) is _____

Trial and error gives the following pairs of values for x and y:

_____

Counting the rows of trees going from north to south, the numbers of rows for three of the groves are: _____

Write an appropriate answer in each blank so that no condition is contradicted.

Hubert's First Watch

Make a table for yourself as follows:

| MONTH | BEGINNING WITH THE MONTH ON THE LEFT | | |
	NUMBER OF DAYS IN THE MONTH	NUMBER OF DAYS IN TWO CONSECUTIVE MONTHS	NUMBER OF DAYS IN THREE CONSECUTIVE MONTHS
January			
February			
March			
April			
May			
June			
July			
August			
September			
October			
November			
December			

Complete the table so that no condition is contradicted.

The Square Table, Part I

Make a seating arrangement around the table for the four men—using the letters A, B, C, and D—so that no condition is contradicted.

The Square Table, Part II

Make a seating arrangement around the table for the four men—using the letters R, S, T, and D—so that no condition is contradicted.

The Two Brothers

Let x be the price in cents for each brother's art object bought; so the brothers spent x times the number of brothers' art objects bought.

The price in cents for each non-brother's art object bought was 2x, so the non-brothers spent 2x times the number of non-brothers' art objects bought; so the brothers spent x times twice the number of non-brothers' art objects bought.

Then the total money spent in cents was x times the number of brothers' art objects bought plus x times twice the number of non-brothers' art objects bought; so the total money spent in cents was x times *the sum of the number of brothers' art objects bought plus twice the number of non-brothers' art objects bought.*

What number(s) can this sum be?

One, Three, or Four

Begin two tables for yourself as follows:

FROM A WINNING POSITION OF	DRAW (1, 3, OR 4)	TO LEAVE A LOSING POSITION OF
1	1	0

FROM A LOSING POSITION OF	IF A PLAYER DRAWS	SHE LEAVES A WINNING POSITION OF
2	1	1

Complete each table—to determine whether drawing from 9 coins is a winning or a losing position—so that no condition is contradicted.

A Timely Death

Make two charts for yourself as follows:

	TO GET TO OSBORN'S CAMP THIS MAN NEEDED		
	MORE THAN 40 MINUTES	AT LEAST 40 MINUTES	LESS THAN 40 MINUTES
Xavier			
Yeoman			
Zenger			

	TO RETURN TO HIS OWN CAMP THIS MAN NEEDED		
	MORE THAN 40 MINUTES	AT LEAST 40 MINUTES	LESS THAN 40 MINUTES
Xavier			
Yeoman			
Zemger			

Place one check mark in each row of each chart—in order to use [6]— so that no condition is contradicted.

Turnabout

In order to discover the digits for C, B, and A, represent the two "good" problems as the following single problem:

$$\begin{array}{r} A\dots B \\ \times \quad C \\ \hline B\dots A \end{array}$$

Then (noting that C × A must be less than 10, neither C nor A can be zero, and C cannot be 1) determine the possible values for C, A, and B so that each letter represents a different digit.

A Week in Burmingham

Using "C" for closed and "O" for open, make a chart for yourself as follows:

	SUN	MON	TUES	WED	THURS	FRI	SAT
Bank	C			C			
Supermarket	C	O	O	C	O	O	O
Department Store	C			C			

Complete the chart so that no condition is contradicted.

Cards on the Table

Because card 6 is the only card that borders on four cards, it would seem to be the easiest card to determine first; then determine the rest of the cards so that no condition is contradicted.

The Murderess

Determine the truth or falsity of each of Statements X, Y, and Z so that no condition is contradicted.

Conversation Stopper

Make a chart for yourself as follows:

Number of people in each group at 8 P.M. = ___a___

Number of people at 8 P.M. (in terms of a) = _____

Number of people in each group at 9 P.M. = ___b___

Number of people at 9 P.M. (in terms of b) = _____ or (in terms of a) =

_____

Number of people in each group at 10 P.M. = ___c___

Number of people at 10 P.M. (in terms of c) = _____ or (in terms of b) =

_____

Number of people in each group at 11 P.M. = ___d___

Number of people at 11 P.M. (in terms of d) = _____ or (in terms of c) =

_____

b = _____, a = _____, c = _____, d = _____

Number of people at 8 P.M. = _____, at 9 P.M. = _____, at 10 P.M. = _____, at 11 P.M. = _____

One person fewer at 8 P.M. = _____, at 9 P.M. = _____, at 10 P.M. = _____, at 11 P.M. = _____

Woman who suspected her husband of infidelity is _____

Complete the chart so that no condition is contradicted.

The Constant Winner

Make a list of the 16 ways the four players could have chosen to take chips from a pile, and record the winner of each game for each way until a different winner occurs for a given way; only one way always yields the same winner for every game through the fifth (and beyond) so that no condition is contradicted.

The Woman Hector Will Marry

Determine the women who have each of the unfortunate traits so that no condition is contradicted.

The Race

Make a chart for yourself as follows:

Of [1], [3], [5], and [7], it is impossible for exactly this number of them to be false: _____.

Of [2], [4], [6], and [8], it is impossible for exactly this number of them to be false: _____ .

SO, these statements must be false: _____.

SO, _____ won the race.

Father and Son

Make two charts for yourself as follows:

	ARNOLD IS	BURTON IS	CLAUDE IS	DENNIS IS
Number of shares bought by	a	b	c	d
Dollars spent per share by	3			
Total number of dollars spent by	3a			
Number of shares bought, if he is the father, by				
Number of shares bought, if he is the son, by				

Father and son together spent _____ dollars.

SO, the two men, who are not father and son, together spent _____ dollars.

SO, _____ cannot be either father or son.

SO, _____ must be either father or son.

SO, based on the two men who are not father and son, one of these equations is true: either _____ + _____ = _____ or _____ + _____ = _____.

SO, the father is _____ and his son is _____.

Complete each chart so that no condition is contradicted.

Murder by Profession

Make a chart for yourself as follows:

Were the victim and the killer from the same family? _____

THEN were the two people at a party from the same family? _____

THEN were the two people at a movie from the same family? _____

   Did the latter two people have the same occupation? _____

SO the two people at a movie were either:

   (ia) _____ and _____ (iia) _____ and _____ (iiia) _____ and _____
   (iva) _____ and _____

THEN the two people at a party were either:

   (ib) _____ and _____ (iib) _____ and _____ (iiib) _____ and _____
   (ivb) _____ and _____

THEN the victim and the killer were (disregarding which was which) either:

   (ic) _____ and _____ (iic) _____ and _____ (iiic) _____ and _____
   (ivc) _____ and _____

THEN—of (i), (ii), (iii), and (iv)—the following three are impossible:

   _____, _____, and _____.

THEN the victim is _____ and the killer is _____.

Complete the chart so that no condition is contradicted.

Six G's

Make a chart for yourself as follows:

F × ABCDE = GGGGGG

F × ABCDE = G × 111,111

Of the whole numbers 2 through 9, 111,111 is divisible by (in other words, yields a whole number when divided by) only _____ and _____.

Is G a multiple of F?
In other words, does G = a × F where a is a whole number? _____

Can F be a multiple of 3?
In other words, can F = b × 3 where b is 1, 2, or 3? _____

Then F = ___

Then ABCDE = G × _____

Then G cannot = _____ , _____ , or _____

Then G = _____

Complete the chart so that each letter in the multiplication represents a different digit.

Two or Three

Begin three tables for yourself as follows:

FROM A LOSING POSITION OF	IF A PLAYER DRAWS	HE LEAVES A WINNING POSITION OF
2	2	0

FROM A WINNING POSITION OF	DRAW (2 OR 3)	TO LEAVE A LOSING POSITION OF
4	2	2

FROM A TIEING POSITION OF	DRAW (2 OR 3)	TO LEAVE A TIEING POSITION OF
1	–	1

Complete each table—to determine whether drawing from twelve coins is a winning, losing, or tieing position—so that no condition is contradicted.

A Week in Cantonville

Using "C" for closed and "O" for open, make a chart for yourself as follows:

	SUN	MON	TUES	WED	THURS	FRI	SAT
Bank	C						
Department Store	C						
Supermarket	C	O	O			O	O

Complete the chart so that no condition is contradicted.

The Bookshelf

Make a chart for yourself as follows:

Let the width of a catalog = c, the width of a dictionary = d, the width of an encyclopedia = e, and the length of the bookshelf = x (all in the same units of measurement).

THEN according to the statement of

Mrs. Astor: _____ + _____ + _____ = x

Mrs. Brice: _____ + _____ + _____ = x

Mrs. Crane: _____ + _____ + _____ = x

Can the pair of equations be correct:

for Mrs. Astor's statement and Mrs. Brice's statement? _____

for Mrs. Astor's statement and Mrs. Crane's statement? _____

for Mrs. Brice's statement and Mrs. Crane's statement? _____

SO the equation for Mrs. _____ 's statement must be incorrect.

Using the two correct equations, can the letter be eliminated:

c? _____   d? _____   e? _____

Will 15 of them exactly fill the shelf:

catalogs? _____   dictionaries? _____   encyclopedias? _____

Complete the chart so that no condition is contradicted.

The Hostess

First determine the trump suit—clubs, diamonds, hearts, or spades—by eliminating the three suits that cannot be the trump suit; then make a chart for yourself as follows:

	ALMA	BESS	CLEO	DINA
Eleventh trick	club (led)	diamond	heart	spade
Twelfth trick				
Thirteenth trick				

Complete the chart—recording which suit cards were led and which suit cards were won—so that no condition is contradicted.

The Rectangular Table

Consider the conditions from the point of view of gender only, from which it follows that men and women could have been seated around the table in only one of two ways. After that, where particular people sat can be determined so that no condition is contradicted.

Deanna's Sister

Noting that all the numbers concerned are positive whole numbers, make a table for yourself as follows:

If P = number of Deanna's pennies, N = number of Deanna's nickels,

Q = number of Deanna's quarters, and T = total cost of candy in cents,

then _____ + _____ + _____ = 13 and _____ + _____ + _____ = T.

If a = number of Althea's candies, b = number of Blythe's candies, and c = number of Carrie's candies, then _____ + _____ + _____ = T and

either _____ = _____, _____ = _____, or _____ = _____.

If d = cost of one gift and G = number of gifts, then _____ × _____ = 480 and _____ + _____ + _____ = G.

Complete the table so that no condition is contradicted and then use it and the following information about odd and even numbers to determine whether a, b, or c is greatest:

The sum of
  two odd numbers is always an even number,
  two even numbers is always an even number,
  an odd number and an even number is always an odd number.

The product of
  two odd numbers is always an odd number,
  two even numbers is always an even number,
  an odd number and an even number is always an even number.

The Cube

Choose one of the four figures that is shown twice on the cube and suppose first that your chosen figure occurs only once and then suppose that your chosen figure occurs twice; record the figure on the bottom face of each view for the three different duplicated figures you are told can occur.

The Club Trick

First determine the suit card played by each player at each trick; then make a chart for yourself as follows:

	ADA	BEA	CYD	DEB
club trick	club	club	club	club
diamond trick				
heart trick				
spade trick				

After completing the chart, find out who led the club by determining who led each of the other three suit cards; do this so that no condition is contradicted.

Twelve C's

Make a chart for yourself as follows:

A does not = 0 or 1; K = 0 and E does not = 0, so B is less than 9,

so A is less than _____, so A = _____, so B = _____ or _____, so E =

_____ or _____, and E = _____, so C = _____, _____, or _____, so C =

_____, so G = _____, so B = _____, so F = _____, so H = _____, so J =

_____. so D = _____.

Write a digit in each blank so that each letter represents a different digit.

John's Ideal Woman

Make a chart for yourself as follows:

	BLUE-EYED?	SLENDER?	BLONDE?	TALL?
Is Adele				
Is Betty				
Is Carol				
Is Doris				

Write "yes," "no," or "maybe" in each box above so that no condition is contradicted.

The L-Shaped Table

The men and women alternate with each other around the L-shaped table and are seated in one of three possible arrangements. Draw three diagrams of the table showing these arrangements; use Mh for the host, Wh for the hostess; use M1, M2, M3, M4, W1, W2, W3, and W4 for the men and women who are guests. Gradually eliminate with lightly written Xs the persons who cannot be the killer or victim, so that no condition is contradicted.

The Tenth Trick

Make a chart for yourself as follows:

Of Hands I, II, III, and IV (regardless of which of two suits is the trump suit):

One pair of partners' hands is _____ and _____.

The other pair of partner's hands is _____ and _____.

Of clubs, diamonds, hearts, and spades:

the trump suit is _____.

Of Art, Bob, Cab, and Don:

Hand I is held by _____.

Hand II is held by _____.

Hand III is held by _____.

Hand IV is held by _____.

At Trick ten, _____ led and _____ won.

At Trick eleven, _____ led and _____ won.

At Trick twelve, _____ led and _____ won.

At Trick thirteen, _____ led and _____ won.

Complete the chart so that no condition is contradicted.

Robert's Position

Make a chart for yourself as follows:

	POLE VAULT	LONG JUMP	HIGH JUMP
Robert's points			
Steven's points			
Thomas's points			

Complete the chart (in one of two correct ways) with numbers of points so that no condition is contradicted.

The Baseball Pennant

Make a chart for yourself as follows:

Let S = Sexton team, T = Treble team, U = Ulster team, and V = Verdue team.

The two teams that could not have won all three games that they each played are _____ and _____.

The only team that could not have lost all three games that it played is _____.

So there are four possible pairs of teams that complete the statement which says: _____ won three games and _____ won 0 games.

The four pairs of teams are I. _____ and _____, II. _____ and _____, III. _____ and _____, IV. _____ and _____.

Checking out each of the four pairs of teams—beginning with the fact that S scored 7 in one game—the solver can determine six scores that can be arranged to form rounds. The six arranged scores are

_____, _____, _____, _____, _____, and _____.

So the _____ won the pennant.

Complete the chart so that no condition is contradicted.

No Cause for Celebration

Make three charts for yourself as follows:

FIRST CHART

Possible boy-girl combinations for the second and third children of each family ("b" stands for brother and "s" stands for sister)

second child	b	b	_____	_____
third child	b	s	_____	_____

Three possible pairs of numbers of b and s for the Browns:

_____ b and _____ s,   _____ b and _____ s,   _____ b and _____ s

Two possible pairs of numbers of b and s for the Joneses:

_____ b and _____ s,   _____ b and _____ s

One possible pair of numbers of b and s for the Smiths:

_____ b and _____ s

THIRD CHART

	NUMBERS OF b and s	BROWN ___ b and ___ s	JONES ___ b and ___ s	SMITH ___ b and ___ s
Insert a "b," "s," or a dash in each blank.	1st	_____	_____	_____
	2nd	_____	_____	_____
	3rd	_____	_____	_____
	4th	_____	_____	_____
	5th	_____	_____	_____
	6th	_____	_____	_____
	7th	_____	_____	_____

Complete each chart so that no condition is contradicted.

Solutions

The Best Player

The best player and the best player's twin are the same age; the best player and the worst player are the same age, from [2]; and the best player's twin and the worst player are two different people, from [1]. Therefore, three of the four people are the same age. So Mr. Scott's son, daughter, and sister must be the same age, because Mr. Scott must be older than both his son and his daughter. Then Mr. Scott's son and daughter must be the twins indicated in [1].

So either Mr. Scott's son or daughter is the best player and Mr. Scott's sister is the worst player. Then, because the best player's twin must be Mr. Scott's son, from [1], *the best player must be Mr. Scott's daughter.*

Mary's Ideal Man

From [1], three of the men are tall and one is not. Then, from [4], Bill and Carl are both tall. Then, from [5], Dave is not tall.

From [2], Dave must have at least one of the required traits; because he is not tall, he must be dark. (Only Mary's ideal man is handsome, but her ideal man is also tall.)

From [1], only two of the men are dark. Then, from [3], Alec and Bill are either both dark or both not dark. Because Dave is dark, Alec and Bill are not dark; otherwise, three men would be dark. From [1], and the fact that Dave is dark, Carl must be dark.

Dave is not tall, Alec and Bill are not dark, and Carl is both tall and dark; so, from [6], *Carl is the only man who could be Mary's ideal man* (so he must be handsome).

In summary: Alec is tall. Bill is tall. Carl is tall, dark, and handsome. Dave is dark.

Middletown

The man who traveled along all the streets in Middletown exactly once (a) had to depart from his home intersection a number of times that was one more than the number of times that he left it, in order to depart from it last, from [3]; and (b) had to arrive at his best friend's home intersection a number of times that was one more than the number of times that he departed from it, in order to arrive at it last, from [3]. The sum of two consecutive (whole) numbers is always an odd number, so this man's home was located at an intersection with an odd number of streets and his best friend's home was located at an intersection with an odd number of streets.

Then, from [1], either Arden visited Duane or Duane visited Arden. From [2], because Arden did not visit Duane and Duane did visit Arden, *Duane must be the man who traveled along all the streets in Middletown exactly ly once*. One possible route for Duane to take through Middletown is shown below.

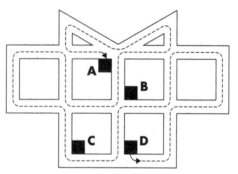

Murder in the Family

The youngest member was not the victim, from [3]; was not the accessory, from [4]; and was not the murderer, from [6]. So the youngest member was the witness.

Then, from [2] and [5], the witness was a woman, so the witness was the daughter; from [1], the accessory was a man; and from [3], the victim was a man. Then, because two men and one woman have been accounted for as to their parts in the murder, the murderer was a woman. So *the murderer was the mother*. From [4], the father was the accessory and the son was the victim.

Three A's

A cannot equal 0 because then M and N would equal 0.

A cannot equal 1 because the product is different from AS.

A cannot equal 2 because a three-digit product would not be possible.

A cannot equal 3 because 4 cannot be carried to A × A.

A cannot equal 4 or 7 because 8 cannot be carried to A × A.

A cannot equal 5 or 6 because then S would have to equal 0, making N equal to S; or S would have to equal 1, making N equal to A.

A cannot equal 9 because then 8 would have to be carried, making A equal to S.

So *A must equal 8*.

Though not necessary for the solution of the problem, the numerical values of S, M, and N can now be determined: since 4 must be carried, S equals 5 or 6; but S cannot equal 6 because then A would equal N. So S is equal to 5. The multiplication is shown below.

$$
\begin{array}{r}
8\ 5 \\
\times\quad 8 \\
\hline
6\ 8\ 0
\end{array}
$$

Everybody Lied

From [II], negating each of the eight false statements results in the following eight true statements:

[1] One of the four killed the psychiatrist.

[2] The psychiatrist was dead when Avery left.

[3] Blake was not the second to arrive.

[4] The psychiatrist was alive when Blake arrived.

[5] Crown was not the third to arrive.

[6] The psychiatrist was dead when Crown left.

[7] The killer arrived after Davis did.

[8] The psychiatrist was alive when Davis arrived.

From [1], [4], [8], [2], and [6], Blake and Davis arrived before Avery and Crown. From [3], Davis must have arrived second; so Blake arrived first. From [5], Avery must have arrived third; so Crown arrived fourth.

The psychiatrist was alive when Davis arrived second but was dead when Avery left third. So, from [1], either Avery or Davis killed the psychiatrist.

From [7], *Avery is the murderer*.

The Triangular Pen

From [1], [2], and [5], the lengths of the sides of the triangular pen are apparently in the ratio of 1 to 2 to 3, but one number is incorrect.

From [3], the incorrect number can be replaced only by a whole number.

From [4], the incorrect number must be replaced by a whole number greater than 3. If either 2 or 3 were replaced by a whole number greater than 3, it would be impossible to construct the pen, because the sum of the lengths of any two sides must be greater than the length of the third side. So 1 is the incorrect number and *the $10 cost for the side of the pen facing the barn must be incorrect*.

If 1 is replaced by a whole number greater than 4, the pen would still be impossible to construct. However, if 1 is replaced by 4, the pen can be constructed. The cost for the side facing the barn must have been $40 instead of $10.

Speaking of Bets

Let a be the amount A had in cents and b be the amount B had in cents before A and B bet. Then, from [1], after they bet, A had 2a cents and B had b−a cents.

Let c be the amount C had in cents before he bet with B. Then, from [2], after B and C bet, B had (b−a)+(b−a) or 2b−2a cents, and C had c−(b−a) or c−b+a cents.

Then, from [3], after C and A bet, C had (c−b+a)+(c−b+a) or 2c−2b+2a cents, and A had 2a−(c−b+a) or a−c+b cents.

From [4], a−c+b = 2b−2a and a−c+b = 2c−2b+2a. The first equation yields: b = 3a−c, and the second equation yields: 3b = a+3c. Multiplying the first of these latter equations by 3 and adding the two equations yields:

6b = 10a or b = 5a/3. Substituting 5a/3 for b (in either b = 3a−c or 3b = a+3c) yields: c = 4a/3.

So A started with a cents, B with 5a/3 cents, and C with 4a/3 cents.

From [5], a cannot be 50 cents because then B and C would have started with fractions of a cent, and 4a/3 cannot be 50 cents because then A and B would have started with fractions of a cent. So 5a/3 is 50 cents and B *is the speaker.*

In summary: A started with 30 cents, B started with 50 cents, and C started with 40 cents.

The Trump Suit

From [1], [2], and [3], the distribution of the four suits is either (a) 1 2 3 7 or (b) 1 2 4 6 or (c) 1 3 4 5.

From [6], combination (c) is eliminated because no suit consists of only two cards. From [5], combination (a) is eliminated because the addition of no two numbers produces a sum of six. So (b) is the correct combination of suits.

From [5], either there are two hearts and four spades or there are four hearts and two spades. From [4], either there are one heart and four diamonds or there are four hearts and one diamond. From [4] and [5] together, there must be four hearts. Then there must be two spades. So *spades is the trump suit.*

In summary: there are four hearts, two spades, one diamond, and six clubs.

Malice and Alice

From [1], [2], and [3], the roles of the five people were as follows: Man and Woman in bar, Killer and Victim on beach, and Child alone.

Then, from [4], either Alice's husband was in the bar and Alice was on the beach, or Alice was in the bar and Alice's husband was on the beach.

If Alice's husband was in the bar, the woman he was with was his daughter, the child who was alone was his son, and Alice and her brother were on the beach. Then either Alice or her brother was the victim; so the other was the killer. But, from [5], the victim had a twin and this twin was innocent. Since Alice and her brother could only be twins to each other, this situation is impossible. Therefore Alice's husband was not in the bar.

So Alice was in the bar. If Alice was in the bar, she was with her brother or her son.

If Alice was with her brother, her husband was on the beach with one of the two children. From [5], the victim could not be her husband, because none of the others could be his twin; so the killer was her husband and the victim was the child he was with. But this situation is impossible, because it contradicts [6]. Therefore Alice was not with her brother in the bar.

So Alice was with her son in the bar. Then the child who was alone was her daughter. Therefore Alice's husband was with Alice's brother on the beach. From previous reasoning, the victim could not be Alice's husband. But the victim could be Alice's brother because Alice could be his twin.

So *Alice's brother was the victim* and Alice's husband was the killer.

A Week in Arlington

From [4] and the fact that all three places are open together on one day each week, the following schedule can be constructed ("C" stands for closed and "O" stands for open):

	1ST	2ND	3RD	4TH	5TH	6TH	7TH
Department Store	C				C	v	O
Supermarket		C	v	C	v	w	O
Bank			C	v	v	C	O

From [1] and [3], each v must be an O; then, from [3], the w must be a C.

	1ST	2ND	3RD	4TH	5TH	6TH	7TH
Department Store	C	y	z	z	C	O	O
Supermarket	x	C	O	C	O	C	O
Bank	z	y	C	O	O	C	O

Then, from [1], the x must be an O; then, from [2], each y must be a C; then, from [1], each z must be an O.

	1ST	2ND	3RD	4TH	5TH	6TH	7TH
Department Store	C	C	O	O	C	O	O
Supermarket	O	C	O	C	O	C	O
Bank	O	C	C	O	O	C	O

From [2], the 2nd day is Sunday; so the 7th day is Friday, and *Friday is the day all three places are open.*

Eunice's Marital Status

From [1] and [2], six couples came to the party. From [3], [4], and [5], if a equals the number of married women present, then a equals the number of married men who came with their wives. Also, $6-a$ equals the number of engaged women present and $6-a$ equals the number of engaged men present. Then, from [6], $6-a$ equals the number of married men present.

If b equals the number of married men who came alone, then the number of married men who came with their wives (a) plus the number of married men who came alone (b) equals the total number of married men present: $a+b = 6-a$. Then the number of married men who came alone (b) equals $6-2a$.

From [7], $6-2a$ equals the number of unattached men who came alone.

From [4], the number of unattached women who came alone, then, equals the number of people who came alone (7) minus the number of married men who came alone ($6-2a$) minus the number of unattached men who came alone: $7 - (6-2a) - (6-2a)$ or $4a-5$.

So a equals the number of married women present, $6-a$ equals the number of engaged women present, and $4a-5$ equals the number of unattached women present.

Because $4a-5$ equals the number of unattached women present, a cannot equal 0 or 1. From [9], Jack was unattached, so a cannot be greater than 2, otherwise the number of unattached men ($6-2a$) would be 0 or less. Therefore a must equal 2.

So there were two married women, four engaged women, and three unattached women at the party.

From [8], *Eunice was an engaged woman.*

A Smart Man

If Brian is smart, then he will pass Chemistry, from [4]. Then, from [1] and [3], Colin will pass Physics, contradicting [6]. So Brian is not smart.

If Colin is smart, then he will pass Physics, from [5]; and he will not pass Chemistry, from [3]. Then, from [1] and [3], Aaron will pass Chemistry, contradicting [2]. So Colin is not smart.

So, from [1], *Aaron is smart.*

Then Colin will not pass Physics, from [6]. So, from [3], Aaron will not pass Chemistry, and Brian and Colin will pass Chemistry. Whether either Aaron or Brian will pass Physics cannot be determined.

The Murderer

From [1], each statement was made by a suspect not mentioned in the statement. Then, from [2], there are only two ways the statements could have been made:

WAY I	WAY II
X. Brad: Adam is innocent, etc.	X. Cole: Adam is innocent, etc.
Y. Cole: Brad is telling the truth.	Y. Adam: Brad is telling the truth.
Z. Adam: Cole is lying.	Z. Brad: Cole is lying.

For Way I: Y supports X; and Z, denying Y, denies X. In effect, the statements become:

X. Brad: Adam is innocent.
Y. Cole: Adam is innocent.
Z. Adam: Adam is guilty.

If "Adam is guilty" is true, then Adam told the truth and is guilty; this situation is impossible, from [3]. If "Adam is innocent" is true, then Brad and Cole told the truth, and one of them is guilty; this situation is impossible, from [3]. So Way I must be incorrect.

For Way II: Z denies X; and Y, supporting Z, denies X. In effect, the statements become:

X. Cole: Adam is innocent.
Y. Adam: Adam is guilty.
Z. Brad: Adam is guilty.

If "Adam is guilty" is true, then Adam told the truth and is guilty; this situation is impossible, from [3]. If "Adam is innocent" is true, then Adam and Brad lied, and one of them is guilty. Because Adam is innocent (even though he lied), *Brad was the murderer.*

The Missing Digit

Because there are four different digits to be added in each column, the largest sum for a column is $9 + 8 + 7 + 6$ or 30. Because I cannot equal zero, no more than 2 can be carried to the left column. Because no more than 2 can be carried to the left column, I cannot equal 3. (If the sum in the right column ended in 3 and the sum in the left column totaled 29 with 2 being carried, obtaining 33 would be impossible.) So I must equal 1 or 2.

If I equals 1, then the right column must add to 11 or 21, while the left column must add to 10 or 9, respectively. Then

$$(B+D+F+H) + (A+C+E+G) + I = 11 + 10 + 1 = 22$$
$$\text{or}$$
$$(B+D+F+H) + (A+C+E+G) + I = 21 + 9 + 1 = 31.$$

But because the sum of the digits 0 through 9 is 45, this situation is impossible; it is impossible because the difference between the sum of the ten digits and the nine digits present in the addition is greater than 9 ($45-22$ or $45-31$). So I must be equal to 2.

Because I equals 2, the right column must add to 12 or 22, while the left column must add to 21 or 20, respectively. Then

$$(B+D+F+H) + (A+C+E+G) + I = 12 + 21 + 2 = 35$$
$$\text{or}$$
$$(B+D+F+H) + (A+C+E+G) + I = 22 + 20 + 2 = 44.$$

The first alternative is impossible, because the difference between the sum of the ten digits and the nine digits present in the addition is greater than 9 ($45-35$). So *the missing digit must be 1* ($45 - 44$).

The existence of at least one addition combination can be confirmed as follows: since zero cannot occur in the left column, by convention, it must occur in the right column. Then three digits must total 22 in the right column. There are only two possibilities for the four digits: either 0, 5, 8, and 9 or 0, 6, 7, and 9. The four digits in the left column, then, are either: 3, 4, 6, and 7 (with 0, 5, 8, and 9 in the right column) or 3, 4, 5, and 8 (with 0, 6, 7, and 9 in the right column). Thus, many addition combinations are possible.

One, Two, or Four

From [II], if a player can win, he *must* win.

From [2] and [3]:

(a) Drawing from one coin, a player loses.

(b) Drawing from two coins, a player wins by taking only one coin, thus putting the other player in the losing position of drawing from one coin.

(c) Drawing from three coins, a player wins by taking two coins, putting the other player in the same losing position as in (b). If he takes only one coin, the other player may take only one coin and win.

(d) Drawing from four coins, a player loses. If he takes one coin he gives the other player the winning position of drawing from three coins. If he takes two coins he gives the other player the winning position of drawing from two coins. If he takes four coins he loses at once. He cannot win because he cannot leave a number of coins that represents a losing position for the other player.

(e) Drawing from five coins, a player wins if he is able to leave a number of coins that represents a losing position for the other player. So if he can leave one coin or four coins for the other player to draw from he wins. Accordingly, he takes four coins, leaving one, or one coin, leaving four.

Reasoning in this manner, one finds that drawings from one, four, seven, and ten coins are losing positions, and drawings from two, three, five, six, eight, and nine coins are winning positions. The tables on the following page summarize how these two sets of drawings can be losing and winning positions, respectively.

FROM A LOSING POSITION OF	IF A PLAYERS DRAWS	HE LEAVES A WINNING POSITION OF
1	1	0
4	1 2 4	3 2 0
7	1 2 4	6 5 3
10	1 2 4	9 8 6

FROM A WINNING POSITION OF	DRAW (1, 2, OR 4)	TO LEAVE A LOSING POSITION OF
2	1	1
3	2	1
5	1 4	4 1
6	2	4
8	1 4	7 4
9	2	7

From [1], there are ten coins. Because drawing from ten coins is a losing position, whoever goes first must lose. Because Austin goes first, from [I], Austin must lose. So *Brooks must win.*

Hubert's First Watch

From [1], no more than 100 days occurred from Hubert's first watch to his last watch.

From [2], the number of days occurring from Hubert's first watch to his last watch must be a multiple of seven.

From [3] and [4], February is not the month Hubert had his first watch because no other month can have the same number of days as February. So more than 28 days occurred from Hubert's first watch to his last watch.

From the previous statements, the number of days occurring from Hubert's first watch to his last watch must be one of the following: 35, 42, 49, 56, 63, 70, 77, 84, 91, or 98.

From these ten possibilities, more than one month and less than four months passed from Hubert's first watch to his last watch. So either two or three months passed from Hubert's first watch to his last watch.

MONTH	BEGINNING WITH THE MONTH ON THE LEFT		
	NUMBER OF DAYS IN THE MONTH	NUMBER OF DAYS IN TWO CONSECUTIVE MONTHS	NUMBER OF DAYS IN THREE CONSECUTIVE MONTHS
January	31	59 or 60	90 or 91
February	28 or 29	59 or 60	89 or 90
March	31	61	92
April	30	61	91
May	31	61	92
June	30	61	92
July	31	62	92
August	31	61	92
September	30	61	91
October	31	61	92
November	30	61	92
December	31	62	90 or 91

In the preceeding table, the only one of the ten possibilities that occurs is 91 days. So 91 days passed from Hubert's first watch to his last watch, resulting in four possible pairs of months for the first and last watches.

	MONTH OF FIRST WATCH	MONTH OF LAST WATCH
I	January (31 days)	April (30 days)
II	April (30 days)	July (31 days)
III	September (30 days)	December (31 days)
IV	December (31 days)	March (31 days)

From [4], *December was the month of Hubert's first watch.*

NOTES: (a) The year in which Hubert had his last watch must be a leap year. (b) The number of days he was *on* watch is 92 days, while the number of days *from* his first watch *to* his last watch is 91 days.

The Student Thief

From [6] and [4], Cobb attended two classes not conducted by the professor. From [6] and [3], Burt attended one class not conducted by the professor. From [6] and [2], Amos attended only classes conducted by the professor.

So, from [1] and [5], Burt and Cobb—but not Amos—attended one other class together that was not conducted by the professor; and Cobb—but not Amos or Burt—attended one other class that was not conducted by the professor. Then, from [7], Burt and Cobb did not attend any other classes together without Amos, and all of Cobb's other classes were attended by at least one of Amos and Burt.

But, from [6] and [7]: one class conducted by the professor that Burt and Cobb attended had to have also been attended by Amos; a second class conducted by the professor had to have been attended by only Amos and Cobb; and a third class conducted by the professor had to have been attended by only Burt. Therefore, from [8], *Burt stole the answer key.*

Let P represent a class conducted by the professor, O represent a class not conducted by the professor, and an x indicate attendance at a class, then the following table summarizes the situation:

	AMOS	BURT	COBB
P		x	
P	x		x
P	x	x	x
O		x	x
O			x

The order of the attendances at the professor's classes does not matter. The order of the other attendances does not matter either.

The Four Groves

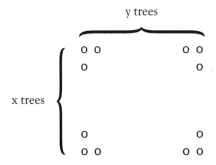

From [1], let x = the number of trees along each of two opposite sides of the three groves mentioned in [3], and let y = the number of trees along each of the other two opposite sides. Then the number of trees on the border is equal to y + y + (x − 2) + (x − 2) or 2y + 2x − 4, and the number of trees in the interior is equal to (x − 2) multiplied by (y − 2).

From [3], $(x - 2)(y - 2) = 2y + 2x - 4$.

Solving for x,

$$xy - 2y - 2x + 4 = 2y + 2x - 4$$
$$xy - 4x = 4y - 8$$
$$x(y - 4) = 4y - 8$$
$$x = (4y - 8)/(y - 4)$$

Dividing $(4y - 8)$ by $(y - 4)$, $x = 4 + 8/(y - 4)$. Thus, y must be greater than 4 and—in order that $8/(y - 4)$ be a positive whole number—y can only be 5, 6, 8, or 12. The corresponding values for x are 12, 8, 6, and 5.

From [2], the apple grove must contain 5 rows, the lemon grove must contain 6 rows, the orange grove must contain 7 rows, and the peach grove must contain 8 rows.

Because it is not possible for a grove with 7 rows to satisfy [3], *the number of trees in the interior of the orange grove does not equal the number of trees on its border.*

In summary, the apple grove has 5 rows of 12 trees each (30 trees on the border and 30 trees in the interior), the lemon grove has 6 rows of 8 trees each (24 trees on the border and 24 trees in the interior), and the peach grove has 8 rows of 6 trees each (the same size as the lemon grove).

The Square Table, Part I

If [6] is false, then Clark did not poison Doyle and statements [1] through [4] are true, from [7]. Then the seating arrangement (using the first letter of each name) was

```
      A
   B     D
      C
```

and, from [2] and [4], respectively, Brent and Alden are innocent. From [8], this situation is impossible.

So [6] is true. Statements [1] and [5] cannot both be true; so, from [6] and [7], either Alden or Clark is guilty and [3] and [4] are true. From [3] and [4], the seating arrangement was one of the following:

In the first arrangement, because [4] is true, Alden is innocent; so, from [6] and [7], Alden told the truth. But [1] is not true for this arrangement, so this arrangement is impossible.

In the second arrangement, because [4] is true, Clark is innocent; so, from [6] and [7], Clark told the truth. But [5] is not true for this arrangement, so this arrangement is impossible.

The third arrangement must be the correct one, because it is the only one possible. Because [4] is true, Alden is innocent. Then *Clark must have poisoned Doyle.*

From [6] and [7], Alden told the truth. So the truth of [1] is consistent with the seating arrangement, and the truth of [2] is consistent with Brent's established innocence. Then [5] must be false, from [7]. That [5] is false is consistent with the seating arrangement.

The Square Table, Part II

If [3] is false, then the seating arrangement (using the first letter of each name) was either:

I	II
R	D
S T	S T
D	R

If [3] is false, then [6] is true, from [7]. So Sid is the poisoner. From [7], statements [1], [2], and [5] are also true.

In the first arrangement [2] is false (Sid is the poisoner), so this arrangement is impossible.

In the second arrangement, it happens that [1], [2], and [5] are true. However, from the statements in Part I the poisoner sat on Doyle's left; in this arrangement, Sid sits on Doyle's right. So this arrangement is impossible.

So [3] is true.

If [1] is true, then [5] is true. If [5] is true, then [1] is true. From [7], [1] and [5] cannot both be false. So [1] and [5] are both true.

Then [1], [3], and [5] are all true.

Because [1], [3], and [5] are all true, the seating arrangement was one of the following:

If [6] is true, Ray or Sid is the poisoner, from [7] and the fact that [5] is true. If [6] is false, Ray or Sid is again the poisoner. Because the poisoner sat on Doyle's left, Ted or Ray is the poisoner, from the third and fourth arrangements. Then the poisoner must be Ray.

So *Ray's wife must be the poisoner's wife.*

It follows that arrangement IV is the correct arrangement. A test of the truth of each statement with this arrangement reveals that only [2] is false.

(The seating arrangement of Part II can be made to correspond to the seating arrangement of Part I by moving each man in Part II's seating arrangement two places around the table. Thus,

```
    A                                  T
  B   D   of Part I corresponds to   S   D   of Part II.)
    C                                  R
```

The Two Brothers

Let x be the price in cents of each art object bought by the two brothers and B be the total number of objects they bought; then they spent Bx cents for their art objects, from [3].

Let 2x be the price in cents of each art object bought by the other four men and M be the total number of art objects they bought; then they spent M2x or 2Mx cents for their art objects, from [4].

Then the total money spent can be represented by the equation $Bx + 2Mx = 100,000$ or $(B + 2M)x = 100,000$, from [5]. Because x must be a whole number of cents (from [1]) and because 100,000 is wholly divisible only by multiples of 2 or 5, B + 2M must be a multiple of either 2 only, 5 only, or both 2 and 5 only.

The total number of art objects bought was $1 + 2 + 3 + 4 + 5 + 6 = 21$. The possible numbers of art objects bought by the two brothers (B) and the corresponding possible numbers of art objects bought by the other four men (M) are listed below. Also listed are the possible values for 2M and 2M + B. (It might be noted that if the same value for B can be gotten by adding more than one pair of numbers—those combinations not checked—there will be more than one possible solution.)

B	M	2M	B + 2M
✓ 1 + 2 = 3	18	36	39
✓ 1 + 3 = 4	17	34	38
$\left.\begin{array}{l} 1 + 4 \\ 2 + 3 \end{array}\right\} = 5$	16	32	37
$\left.\begin{array}{l} 1 + 5 \\ 2 + 4 \end{array}\right\} = 6$	15	30	36
$\left.\begin{array}{l} 1 + 6 \\ 2 + 5 \\ 3 + 4 \end{array}\right\} = 7$	14	28	35
$\left.\begin{array}{l} 2 + 6 \\ 3 + 5 \end{array}\right\} = 8$	13	26	34
$\left.\begin{array}{l} 3 + 6 \\ 4 + 5 \end{array}\right\} = 9$	12	24	33
✓ 4 + 6 = 10	11	22	32
✓ 5 + 6 = 11	10	20	31

Of the nine possible values for B + 2M, just the value 32 is a multiple of 2 only, 5 only, or both 2 and 5 only.

The corresponding value for B is 10, and 10 is the sum of only one pair of numbers: 4 and 6. Therefore, from [2], *Dwight and Farley are brothers.*

To find the cost of the art objects in cents, substitute 32 for B + 2M:

$$(B + 2M)x = 100,000$$
$$32x = 100,000$$
$$x = 3,125$$
$$2x = 6,250$$

Checking the solution:

$$(4 + 6 = 10) \qquad 10 \times 3,125 = 31,250$$
$$(1 + 2 + 3 + 5 = 11) \qquad 11 \times 6,250 = 68,750$$
$$\overline{ 100,000}$$

One, Three, or Four

From [II], if a player *can* win, she *must* win.

From [2] and [3]:

(a) Drawing from one coin, a player wins.

(b) Drawing from two coins, a player loses. She must take one coin, thus putting the other player in the winning position of drawing from one coin.

(c) Drawing from three coins, a player wins because if she takes all three coins she wins at once and if she takes one coin she puts the other player in the losing position of drawing from two coins.

(d) Drawing from four coins, a player wins by taking all four coins. If she takes one coin she gives the other player the winning position of drawing from three coins. If she takes three coins she gives the other player the winning position of drawing from one coin.

(e) Drawing from five coins, a player wins if she is able to leave a number of coins that represents a losing position for the other player. So if she can leave two coins for the other player to draw from she wins. Accordingly, she takes three coins.

Reasoning in this manner, one finds that drawings from two, seven, and nine coins are losing positions, and drawings from one, three, four, five, six, and eight coins are winning positions. The following tables summarize how these two sets of drawings can be winning and losing positions, respectively:

FROM A WINNING POSITION OF	DRAW (1, 3, OR 4)	TO LEAVE A LOSING POSITION OF
1	1	0
3	$\begin{cases} 1 \\ 3 \end{cases}$	$\begin{cases} 2 \\ 0 \end{cases}$
4	4	0
5	3	2
6	4	2
8	1	7

FROM A LOSING POSITION OF	IF A PLAYER DRAWS	SHE LEAVES A WINNING POSITION OF
2	1	1
7	$\begin{cases} 1 \\ 3 \\ 4 \end{cases}$	$\begin{cases} 6 \\ 4 \\ 3 \end{cases}$
9	$\begin{cases} 1 \\ 3 \\ 4 \end{cases}$	$\begin{cases} 8 \\ 6 \\ 5 \end{cases}$

From [1], there are nine coins. Because drawing from nine coins is a losing position, whoever goes first must lose. Because Audrey goes first, from [1], Audrey must lose. So *Bonita must win.*

A Timely Death

From [1], Osborn was shot in his camp before 10:30. Therefore (if one of the three men shot Osborn), from [2], [4], and [6], it is not possible that Osborn was shot in his camp after 9:50 because then each of the three men would have had only 75 minutes to make the round trip to and from Osborn's camp: Xavier had from 9:40 to 10:55, Yeoman had from 9:45 to 11:00, and Zenger had from 9:50 to 11:05.

From [1], Osborn died instantly; from [6], Osborn replied to Wilson's call at 9:15. So (if one of the three men shot Osborn) Osborn was shot after 9:15 and no later than 9:50.

[6] allows each of the three men a maximum of 85 minutes to make the round trip to and from Osborn's camp: Xaxier had from 8:15 to 9:40, Yeoman had from 8:20 to 9:45, and Zenger had from 8:25 to 9:50. So,

If Xavier shot Osborn, he must have done so before 9:40;

If Yeoman shot Osborn, he must have done so before 9:45; and

If Zenger shot Osborn, he must have done so before 9:50.

But, from [3], [4], and [5]:

Xavier required more than 40 minutes to get to Osborn's camp;

Yeoman required at least 40 minutes to get to Osborn's camp, and required at least 40 minutes to return to his own camp;

Zenger required more than 40 minutes to return to his own camp.

If Yeoman shot Osborn, he must have left Osborn's camp by 9:05, at least 40 minutes before replying to Wilson's second call. If Zenger shot Osborn, he must have left Osborn's camp before 9:10, more than 40 minutes before replying to Wilson's second call. So, if Yeoman or Zenger shot Osborn, a reply from Osborn at 9:15 would not have been possible— because Osborn, having died instantly, could not have replied.

However, if Xavier shot Osborn, he had only to arrive at Osborn's camp after 8:55—more then 40 minutes after replying to Wilson's first call. So, if Xavier left Osborn's camp after 9:15, he still may have had enough time to return to his own camp. So *Xavier was not eliminated from Wilson's suspicion.*

Turnabout

A, B, and C occur in the same positions in the three problems. So, from [2], two problems can be considered as one problem with an indeterminate number of letters occuring between A and B. Because two products contain in reverse order the same digits as the numbers multiplied by C, two problems can be represented as the following single problem.

$$
\begin{array}{r}
A \ldots\ldots B \\
\times \quad C \\
\hline
B \ldots\ldots A
\end{array}
$$

Then, from [1], the following reasoning can be applied to this single problem:

C × A must be less than 10, neither C nor A can be zero, and C cannot be 1. (Though A is not zero by convention, because it begins a number, it is also impossible for A to be zero.) So the following values for C and A are possible:

	C	A		C	A		C	A
(1)	2	1	(5)	3	2	(9)	6	1
(2)	2	3	(6)	4	1	(10)	7	1
(3)	2	4	(7)	4	2	(11)	8	1
(4)	3	1	(8)	5	1	(12)	9	1

C × B must end in A; so if C is even, A must be even also. This consideration eliminates (1), (2), (6), (9), and (11). If C is 5, C × B can only end in 5 or 0, not 1; so (8) is eliminated. If C is 9, B must be 9 in order that A be 1; but C and B cannot both be 9, so (12) is eliminated. Multiplying the remaining possible values of C by 1 through 9 to get a value for B, in order that A be the value listed, one arrives at the following combinations:

	C	B	A
(3)	2	7	4
(4)	3	7	1
(5)	3	4	2

	C	B	A
(7a)	4	3	2
(7b)	4	8	2
(10)	7	3	1

C × A must be less than or equal to B; so (3), (5), (7a), and (10) are eliminated. For (4) and (7b), one arrives at these two possible partial multiplications:

$$
\begin{array}{rl}
(4) & 1\,R\ldots 7 \\
    & \times \quad 3 \\
    \hline
    & 7\,\ldots\ldots 1
\end{array}
\qquad
\begin{array}{rl}
(7b) & 2\,R\ldots 8 \\
     & \times \quad 4 \\
     \hline
     & 8\,\ldots\ldots 2
\end{array}
$$

In (4) it is impossible to carry as much as 4 from 3 × R to 3 × 1 to get 7; so (4) is eliminated. So (7b) is the only possible partial multiplication, and A = 2, B = 8, and C = 4 in the two problems mentioned in [2].

In (7b), 3 is carried from 4 × 8. So, if R occurs in the product, R cannot equal zero. R cannot equal 2 because A = 2. R cannot equal more than 2 because nothing is carried from 4 × R to 4 × 2. So, if R occurs in the product, R = 1.

In order for the digits in the product to be the same as the digits in the number multiplied by C, it is necessary for R to be equal to 1. If 1 is substituted for R in problem I, the multiplication becomes:

$$
\begin{array}{r}
2\ 1\ 8 \\
\times \quad 4 \\
\hline
8\ 7\ 2
\end{array}
$$

The product 872 is not the reverse of 218, so from [2], *Problem I is the problem in which the digits in the product are not the same as the digits in the number multiplied by C.*

Problems II and III can be completed as follows:

In Problem II,

$$
\begin{array}{r}
2\ 1\ S\ 8 \\
\times\qquad 4 \\
\hline
8\ S\ 1\ 2
\end{array}
\qquad \text{, S so must be 7:} \qquad
\begin{array}{r}
2\ 1\ 7\ 8 \\
\times\qquad 4 \\
\hline
8\ 7\ 1\ 2
\end{array}
$$

In Problem III,

$$
\begin{array}{r}
2\ 1\ S\ T\ 8 \\
\times\qquad 4 \\
\hline
8\ T\ S\ 1\ 2
\end{array}
\qquad \text{, T so must be 7:} \qquad
\begin{array}{r}
2\ 1\ S\ 7\ 8 \\
\times\qquad 4 \\
\hline
8\ 7\ S\ 1\ 2
\end{array}
$$

Then S must be 9:

$$
\begin{array}{r}
2\ 1\ 9\ 7\ 8 \\
\times\qquad 4 \\
\hline
8\ 7\ 9\ 1\ 2
\end{array}
$$

A Week in Burmingham

From [3] and [4], the following schedule can be constructed ("C" stands for closed and "O" stands for open):

	SUN	MON	TUES	WED	THURS	FRI	SAT
Bank	C			C			
Supermarket	C	O	O	C	O	O	O
Department Store	C			C			

Then: from [2] and [5], the department store is closed on either Thursday or Monday and is open on the other four days; from [2] and [6], the department store is closed on either Monday or Friday and is open on the other four days. So, from [5] and [6], the department store must be closed on Monday and open on the other four days.

	SUN	MON	TUES	WED	THURS	FRI	SAT
Bank	C	y	C	C	x	x	x
Supermarket	C	O	O	C	O	O	O
Department Store	C	C	O	C	O	O	O

Then, from [1], each x must be a C. Because the bank was open on the day I went into Burmingham, the y must be an O. So *I went into the town of Burmingham on Monday.*

Cards on the Table

If card 6 were a Jack, then—from [1]—card 3 would be a Queen between two Kings (cards 2 and 4) and [2] and [6] could not both be satisfied. So card 6 is not a Jack.

If card 6 were the Ace mentioned in [4], then—from [5]—[1] could not be satisfied. So card 6 is not the Ace.

If card 6 were a Queen, then—from [3]—[2] could not be satisfied. So card 6 is not a Queen.

Then card 6 is a King. Then, from [5], the Ace is either card 1, 2, or 3.

If card 1 were the Ace, then—from [5]—[1] could not be satisfied. So card 1 is not the Ace.

If card 2 or card 3 were the Ace, then—from [1]—only card 4 could be a Queen between two Kings; then—from [2]—cards 5 and 7 would be Jacks; then—from [6]—card 8 would be a King.

$$
\begin{array}{ccc}
 & K & \\
2 & 3 & Q \\
 J & K & J \\
 & K &
\end{array}
$$

If card 2 were the Ace, then: card 3 could not be a Jack or a Queen—from [3]; could not be an Ace—from [4]; and could not be a King—from [5]. Thus, the identity of card 3 could not satisfy [7]. So card 2 is not the Ace.

Therefore, *card 3 is the Ace.* Then—from [4]—card 2 is not an Ace and—from [5]—card 2 is not a King. Thus—from [7]—card 2 is either a Queen or a Jack; exactly which one cannot be determined.

The Murderess

Because each of Statements X, Y, and Z refers to a different woman, the innocent one did not make all three statements; otherwise, she would have spoken of herself, contradicting [1]. So the innocent one made either one statement or two statements, from [2].

If the innocent one made only one statement, then only that statement is true and the other two statements are false, from [3]. But this situation is impossible: if any two of these statements are false, then the remaining one has to be false—as shown by the following analysis.

(a) If X and Y are the false statements, then Anna is the accomplice and Babs is the murderess. So Cora must be the innocent one, making Z false.

(b) If X and Z are the false statements, then Anna is the accomplice and Cora is the innocent one. So Babs must be the murderess, making Y false.

(c) If Y and Z are the false statements, then Babs is the murderess and Cora is the innocent one. So Anna must be the accomplice, making [1] false.

Therefore, the innocent woman made two statements. From [1], the two true statements were made by the only woman not referred to in the two statements—as shown below.

(d) If Y and Z are the true statements, then they were made by Anna. Then Anna is the innocent one. But X, being false, identifies Anna as the accomplice. This situation is impossible.

(e) If X and Z are the true statements, then they were made by Babs. Then Babs is the innocent one. But Y, being false, identifies Babs as the murderess. This situation is impossible.

(f) So X and Y are the true statements and they were, therefore, made by Cora. Then Cora is the innocent one. The falsity of Z is consistent with this conclusion.

Because Cora is the innocent one and X is true, Babs is the accomplice. Then *Anna is the murderess*. Y, being true, is consistent with this conclusion.

It cannot be determined whether Anna or Babs made Statement Z.

Conversation Stopper

Let a = the number of people in each group at 8 P.M. Then, from [1], there were 5a people at the party at 8 P.M. Let b = the number of people in each group at 9 P.M. Then, from [2], there were 4b people at the party at 9 P.M. Because only two people arrived between 8 P.M. and 9 P.M., from [1] and [2], 5a + 2 = 4b.

Let c = the number of people in each group at 10 P.M. Then, from [3], there were 3c people at the party at 10 P.M. Because only two people arrived between 9 P.M. and 10 P.M., from [2] and [3], 4b + 2 = 3c.

Let d = the number of people in each group at 11 P.M. Then, from [4], there were 2d people at the party at 11 P.M. Because only two people arrived between 10 P.M. and 11 P.M., from [3] and [4], 3c + 2 = 2d.

Trial and error yields the following values for a, b, and c in the first and second equations (a cannot be greater than 20, from [1]):

5a + 2 = 4b		4b + 2 = 3c	
a	b	b	c
2	3	1	2
6	8	4	6
10	13	7	10
14	18	10	14
18	23	13	18
		16	22
		19	26
		22	30

Because b must have the same value in both equations, b = 13; then a = 10 and c = 18. Because c = 18, d = 28 in the third equation.

So at 8 P.M. there were 50 people, at 9 P.M. there were 52 people, at 10 P.M. there were 54 people, and at 11 P.M. there were 56 people.

From [1], [5], and [6], if Amelia were the woman to arrive an hour after her husband, the number of people present at 8 P.M. would be 49. From [2], [5], and [6], if Brenda were the woman to arrive an hour after her husband, the number of people present at 9 P.M. would be 51. From [3], [5], and [6], if Cheryl were the woman to arrive an hour after her husband, the number of people present at 10 P.M. would be 53. From [4], [5], and [6], if Denise were the woman to arrive an hour after her husband, the number of people present at 11 P.M. would be 55.

Of the four numbers of people—49, 51, 53, and 55—53 people is the only number of people not divisible into smaller groups containing an equal number of people (the number of people in each group must be at least two for conversation to take place).

So, from [3] and [6], *Cheryl is the woman who suspected her husband of infidelity*.

The Constant Winner

From [2], there are 16 ways the four players could have chosen to take chips from a pile. These ways are listed below. Using [1], suppose eight chips are in a pile, then 10 chips, then 12 chips, then 14 chips, then 16 chips, then 18 chips, then 20 chips. Using [3] and [4], record the winner of each game for each combination until a different winner occurs for a given combination. The winners are recorded below alongside the combinations. Combination nine: 1, 2, 2, 1 is the only combination yielding the same winner, Don, for each game. For all other even numbers of chips, Don will always win with this combination. So *Don won every game*.

	ABE	BEN	CAL	DON	NUMBERS OF CHIPS						
					8	10	12	14	16	18	20
1.	1	1	1	1	Don	Ben					
2.	2	1	1	1	Ben	Don					
3.	1	2	1	1	Ben	Don					
4.	1	1	2	1	Don	Don	Ben				
5.	1	1	1	2	Cal	Don					
6.	2	2	1	1	Abe	Ben					
7.	2	1	2	1	Abe	Don					
8.	2	1	1	2	Abe	Cal					
9.	1	2	2	1	Don	Don	Don	Don	Don	Don	Don
10.	1	2	1	2	Cal	Cal	Don				
11.	1	1	2	2	Ben	Cal					
12.	1	2	2	2	Abe	Ben					
13.	2	1	2	2	Ben	Ben	Cal				
14.	2	2	1	2	Cal	Cal	Cal	Don			
15.	2	2	2	1	Don	Don	Don	Don	Abe		
16.	2	2	2	2	Don	Abe					

The Woman Hector Will Marry

If Bernice nags, then—from [3] and [5]—all three women nag. If Claudia nags, then—from [5]—Annette nags. Annette may be the only woman who nags. So, from [7], the possible combinations for nagging women are BCA, CA, and A (B represents Bernice, C represents Claudia, and A represents Annette).

From [1] and [4], either both Annette and Bernice talk a lot or neither of them talk a lot. Claudia may or may not talk a lot. So, from [7], the possible combinations for women who talk a lot are: BCA, AB, and C.

If Annette is stubborn, then—from [2]—Claudia is stubborn. If Bernice is stubborn, then—from [6]—Claudia is not stubborn. So Annette and Bernice cannot both be stubborn. Claudia may be the only woman who is stubborn or Bernice may be the only woman who is stubborn. So, from [7], the possible combinations for women who are stubborn are: AC, C, and B.

From [9], the two women mentioned in [8] possess more than one of the unfortunate traits in common. Then those two women possess either two or three of the same unfortunate traits. Those two women cannot be Bernice and Claudia, from [2] and [6]—either Bernice is stubborn or Claudia is stubborn, but not both and not neither. Those two women cannot be Annette and Bernice because then Claudia will have either two or three unfortunate traits. So Annette and Claudia are those two women and *Bernice is the woman Hector will marry*.

The only possible distribution of traits is: Nags–CA, Talks a lot–BCA, Is stubborn–AC. Bernice's only unfortunate trait is Talks a lot.

Father and Son

Let the number of shares bought by Arnold be a, by Burton be b, by Claude be c, and by Dennis be d. Then the equation that represents the total number of dollars spent, from [1] and [4], is $3a + 4b + 6c + 8d = 161$.

Then—from [2] and [3]—if either Arnold or Burton is the father and the other of the two is his son, (i) $96 + 6c + 8d = 161$ and $6c + 8d = 65$. Similarly, for Arnold and Claude, (ii) $4b + 8d = 65$; for Arnold and Dennis, (iii) $4b + 6c = 65$; for Burton and Claude, (iv) $3a + 8d = 65$; for Burton and Dennis, (v) $3a + 6c = 65$; for Claude and Dennis, (vi) $3a + 4b = 65$.

NOTES: [I] Each of the letters a, b, c, and d represents a positive whole number. [II] If a whole number divides exactly into two of the three terms in an equation, then that whole number must divide exactly into the third term. From [I] and [II], (i), (ii), and (iii) are impossible because 65 is not exactly divisible by 2; (v) is impossible because 65 is not exactly divisible by 3. In (iv), either b was 6 (the smallest number of shares) while c was 12 (the greatest number of shares), or b was 18 (the greatest number of shares) while c was 4 (the smallest number of shares); the only possible whole number pairs for a and d are, respectively, 3 and 7, 11 and 4, 19 and 1; so (iv) is impossible.

In (vi), either c was 4 (the smallest number of shares) while d was 9 (the greatest number of shares), or c was 12 (the greatest number of shares) while d was 3 (the smallest number of shares). The only possible whole number pairs for a and b are, respectively, 3 and 14, 7 and 11, 11 and 8, 15 and 5, 19 and 2; so (vi) is impossible if c were 4 and d were 9, but (vi) is possible if c were 12 and d were 3. So *Claude is the father and Dennis is his son.* The two sets of possible values are a = 7, b = 11, c = 12, d = 3; and a = 11, b = 8, c = 12, d = 3.

The Race

If two of [1], [3], [5], and [7] are true, then a third one has to be true; so of [1], [3], [5], and [7], it is impossible for exactly two of them to be false. If three of [2], [4], [6], and [8] are false, then the fourth has to be false; so of [2], [4], [6], and [8], it is impossible for exactly three of them to be false.

Therefore, either one, three, or four of [1], [3], [5], and [7] are false (at least one has to be false), and either none, one, two, or four of [2], [4], [6], and [8] are false.

From [I], six statements are false altogether. There is only one way to get a total of six by adding two of these numbers of possible false statements: four plus two. Therefore, [1], [3], [5], and [7] are all false and two of [2], [4], [6], and [8] are false.

If [2] is false, Alan won the race, which contradicts [II]. So [2] is true. Then, either: [2] and [4] are true, [2] and [6] are true, or [2] and [8] are true.

If [2] and [4] are true, then [6] and [8] are false, and the order in which the men finished the race is BACD (the letters are the first letters of the names of the four men). But this order contradicts [5] as false, so it is not the correct one.

If [2] and [8] are true, then [4] and [6] are false, and the order in which the men finished the race is DBCA. But this order contradicts [3] as false, so it is not the correct one.

So [2] and [6] must be true, which implies that [4] and [8] are false, and the order in which the men finished the race is CBAD. Therefore, *Clay won the race*.

Murder by Profession

From [3], the victim and the killer were either both Whites or both Blacks. Then, from [4], the two people at a party were either both Whites or both Blacks—but they were not from the same family as the victim and the killer.

So the two people at a movie were from different families (a White and a Black); from [2], these people had the same occupation. Thus, the people at a movie were either (i) Cass and Earl, (ii) Cass and Faye, (iii) Alex and Dean, or (iv) Bell and Dean.

Then:

	(I)	(II)	(III)	(IV)
AT MOVIE	Cass & Earl	Cass & Faye	Alex & Dean	Bell & Dean

Then, because there are four possibilities, from [1] (the doctor and the lawyer must be from the same family):

	(I)	(II)	(III)	(IV)
AT PARTY	Dean & Faye	Dean & Earl	Bell & Cass	Alex & Cass

Then, because there are only two possibilities left for the victim and the killer:

	(I)	(II)	(III)	(IV)
IN PARK	Alex & Bell	Alex & Bell	Earl & Faye	Earl & Faye

From [4], (ii) and (iii) are impossible (because the killer and the victim are of opposite sex, the two people at a party must be of opposite sex too).

(iv) satisfies [5] with Faye as the victim (Faye and Alex have different occupations, while Earl and Cass have the same occupation) and Earl as the killer; but, from [6a], while only Dean can be the ex-spouse of Cass,

101

from [6b], Bell and Alex cannot have been same-sex roommates. So (iv) is impossible.

(i) satisfies [5] with Alex as the victim (Alex and Faye have different occupations, while Bell and Dean have the same occupation) and Bell as the killer; from [6a], Cass must be the ex-spouse of Dean and, from [6b], Earl and Dean must have been the same-sex roommates. So only (i) is possible and *Bell was the killer.*

Six G's

F × ABCDE = GGGGGG. So F × ABCDE = G × 111111.

Of the numbers 2 through 9, 111111 is divisible exactly by only 3 and 7. So F × ABCDE = G × 3 × 7 × 5291.

If G is a multiple of F, then ABCDE would be a number containing the same digit six times. So G is not a multiple of F.

Then:

(a) F does not equal zero; otherwise G would equal zero and, therefore, would be a multiple of F.

(b) F does not equal 1; otherwise G would be a multiple of F.

(c) F does not equal 2; otherwise G would be a multiple of 2 (for an exact division) and, therefore, a multiple of F.

(d) F does not equal 4; otherwise G would be a multiple of 4 (for an exact division) and, therefore, a multiple of F.

(e) F does not equal 8; otherwise G would be 8 also (for an exact division) and, therefore, a multiple of F.

(f) F does not equal 5; otherwise G would be 5 also (for an exact division) and, therefore, a multiple of F.

(g) If F = 3, then ABCDE = G × 7 × 5291 = G × 37037. The presence of a zero in 37037 indicates that the product of any single digit times this number will result in duplicate digits for ABCDE. So F does not equal 3.

(h) If F = 6, then 2 × ABCDE = G × 7 × 5291 = G × 37037. G, then, is a multiple (M) of 2, that is, G = 2 × M. Then ABCDE = M × 37037. By the reasoning in (g), F does not equal 6.

(i) If F = 9, then 3 × ABCDE = G × 7 × 5291 = G × 37037. G, then, is a multiple (M) of 3, that is, G = 3 × M. Then ABCDE = M × 37037. By the reasoning in (g), F does not equal 9.

(j) So F = 7. Then ABCDE = G × 3 × 5291 = G × 15873. Because there are seven different digits involved, G does not equal 1, 5, or 7. Because ABCDE contains only five digits, G does not equal 8 or 9. Because F does not equal zero, G does not equal zero. So G equals 2, 3, 4, or 6.

The four possibilities are F = 7, G = 2, ABCDE = 31746
F = 7, G = 3, ABCDE = 47619
F = 7, G = 4, ABCDE = 63492
F = 7, G = 6, ABCDE = 95238

Only the last one of these possibilities results in seven different digits. The multiplication, then, is

$$
\begin{array}{r}
9\ 5\ 2\ 3\ 8 \\
\times\qquad\ \ 7 \\
\hline
6\ 6\ 6\ 6\ 6\ 6
\end{array}
$$

Two or Three

From [II], if a player *can* win, he *must* win; if a player *can* force a tie (assuming he cannot win), then he *must* force a tie.

From [2] and [3]:

(a) If a pile contains only one coin, then the game must end in a tie because neither player can draw from the pile.

(b) Drawing from two coins, a player loses because he must take the two coins.

(c) If a pile contains three coins, then the game must end in a tie. If a player takes three coins he loses. If he takes two coins, the other player cannot draw.

(d) Drawing from four coins, a player wins by taking two coins, thus putting the other player in the losing position of drawing from two coins. If he takes three coins, then the game ends in a tie.

(e) Drawing from five coins, a player wins if he is able to leave a number of coins that represents a losing position for the other player. Accordingly, he takes three coins, putting the other player in the losing position of drawing from two coins.

(f) If a pile contains six coins, then the game must end in a tie. A player draws three coins, leaving three coins that represent a tieing position. If a player draws two coins, he gives the other player the winning position of drawing from four coins.

Reasoning in this manner, one finds that drawings from two, seven, and twelve coins are losing positions; drawings from four, five, nine, and ten coins are winning positions; and drawings from one, three, six, eight, and eleven coins are tieing positions. The following tables summarize how these three sets of drawings can be losing, winning, and tieing positions, respectively.

FROM A LOSING POSITION OF	IF A PLAYER DRAWS	HE LEAVES A WINNING POSITION OF
2	2	0
7	$\begin{cases} 2 \\ 3 \end{cases}$	$\begin{cases} 5 \\ 4 \end{cases}$
12	$\begin{cases} 2 \\ 3 \end{cases}$	$\begin{cases} 10 \\ 9 \end{cases}$

FROM A WINNING POSITION OF	DRAW (2 OR 3)	TO LEAVE A LOSING POSITION OF
4	2	2
5	3	2
9	2	7
10	3	7

FROM A TIEING POSITION OF	DRAW (2 OR 3)	TO LEAVE A TIEING POSITION OF
1	—	1
3	2	1
6	3	3
8	2	6
11	3	8

From [1], there are twelve coins. Because drawing from twelve coins is a losing position, whoever goes first must lose. Because Armand goes first, from [I], Armand must lose. So *Buford must win.*

A Week in Cantonville

From [5], all three places are closed on Sunday. So, from [1] and [8], the supermarket is open on Monday, Tuesday, Friday, and Saturday. Then, from [2] and [7], the department store is not closed on both Saturday and Monday; likewise, from [3] and [6], the bank is not closed on both Saturday and Monday.

So, from [9] and previous reasoning, either:

(A) the bank is the only place closed on Saturday and the department store is the only place closed on Monday, or

(B) the department store is the only place closed on Saturday and the bank is the only place closed on Monday.

The following schedule can now be constructed ("C" stands for closed, "O" stands for open, "x" stands for either open or closed, and "y" stands for the opposite of what x stands for):

	SUN	MON	TUES	WED	THURS	FRI	SAT
Bank	C	x	y	x	y	x	y
Department Store	C	y		z			x
Supermarket	C	O	O			O	O

If y represents C, then x represents O and, from [7], z must represent O. This situation is impossible, from [4] ([4] cannot be satisfied). So, x represents C and y represents O. Then—from [7]—z must represent C, so that the supermarket is open on the remaining days:

	SUN	MON	TUES	WED	THURS	FRI	SAT
Bank	C	C	O	C	O	C	O
Department Store	C	O	O	C	O	O	C
Supermarket	C	O	O			O	O

So *Tuesday must be the day all three places are open.*

From [1] and the fact that all three places are open on only one day each week, the supermarket must be closed on Thursday and open on Wednesday.

The Bookshelf

Using [4] (all measurements in the same units), let

c = the width of a catalog

d = the width of a dictionary

e = the width of an encyclopedia

x = the length of the bookshelf

Then, according to each assistant's statement:

(A) Astor: $2c + 3d + 3e = x$

(B) Brice: $4c + 3d + 2e = x$

(C) Crane: $4c + 4d + 3e = x$

Subtracting A from C: $2c + d = 0$ and $d = -2c$, which is impossible.

Subtracting B from C: $d + e = 0$ and $d = -e$, which is impossible.

Subtracting B from A: $-2c + e = 0$ and $e = 2c$, which *is* possible.

Because the use of C with each of A and B results in an impossible situation, Mrs. Crane was incorrect. So—from [1]—equations A and B are correct, and $e = 2c$.

From [3], if 15 encyclopedias can exactly fill the shelf, then so can 30 catalogs. Therefore, from [2], the encyclopedias cannot exactly fill the shelf.

If 15 dictionaries can fill the shelf (that is, if $x = 15d$), then using A (or B) and $e = 2c$:

$$(A)\ 2c + 3d + 3e = x$$
$$e + 3d + 3e = x$$
$$3d + 4e = 15d$$
$$4e = 12d$$
$$e = 3d$$

From [3], if 15 dictionaries can exactly fill the shelf, then so can 5 encyclopedias. Therefore, from [2], the dictionaries cannot exactly fill the shelf.

So the catalogs can exactly fill the shelf.

Using A (or B), $e = 2c$, and $x = 15c$:

$$(A)\ 2c + 3d + 3e = x$$
$$2c + 3d + 6c = x$$
$$3d + 8c = x$$
$$3d + 8c = 15c$$
$$3d = 7c$$
$$d = 2\tfrac{1}{3}\,c$$

If 15 catalogs can exactly fill the shelf, then the encyclopedias cannot;

using e = 2c, 7½ encyclopedias would fill the same space. The dictionaries cannot exactly fill the shelf; using d = 2⅓ c, 6½ dictionaries would fill the same space.

The Hostess

Clubs is not trump; otherwise, from [1] and [4], Alma would have led more than once, which contradicts [3].

Hearts is not trump; otherwise, from [2] and [4], the hostess would have won more than once, which contradicts [5].

From [1], no one followed Alma's lead of a club, indicating no one else had a club; yet, from [4], a club was played at each trick. So Alma must have had three clubs. Because a trump won each of the last three tricks and clubs cannot be trump, Alma did not win any of the tricks. From [5], each of the other three women won one trick. Therefore, each of the other three women had one trump.

Spades (black cards) is not trump; otherwise, no one had three red cards, which contradicts [6].

So diamonds is trump.

Then, from [1], Bess won at trick number eleven and led at trick number twelve.

From [2], the hostess won the twelfth trick (with a trump) and led a heart; so, from [4], hearts was not led at trick number twelve.

Diamonds could not have been led at trick number twelve because Bess would have won more than one trick, which contradicts [5] (having won at trick number eleven, she would also have won at trick number twelve, from [4]).

Clubs could not have been led at trick number twelve because Alma had all the clubs and, from [3], she led only once (at trick number eleven, from [1]).

So spades was led by Bess at trick number twelve. The table below records the suits known to have been played by each woman so far.

	ALMA	BESS	CLEO	DINA
Eleventh trick	club (led)	diamond (won)	heart	spade
Twelfth trick	club	spade (led)		
Thirteenth trick	club			

Because Alma, Bess, and Dina all had black cards at this point, it follows—from [6]—that the hostess' partner must be Cleo. So Cleo could not have been the hostess, and so—from [2]—did not play a diamond (trump) when Bess led a spade at trick number twelve.

So Dina must have played a diamond (trump) when Bess led a spade at trick number twelve. Then, from [2], *Dina was the hostess*.

The analysis may be continued. From [2], Dina led a heart at trick number thirteen. So—from [4]—Cleo played a heart at trick number twelve, and—from [5]—Cleo played a diamond (trump) at trick number thirteen. Then, from [4], Bess played a spade at trick number thirteen. The completed table is shown below.

	ALMA	BESS	CLEO	DINA
Eleventh trick	club (led)	diamond (won)	heart	spade
Twelfth trick	club	spade (led)	heart	diamond (won)
Thirteenth trick	club	spade	diamond (won)	heart (led)

The Rectangular Table

From [4], three men sat next to each other and one man sat between two women (two men could not have sat next to each other at two different places, and four men could not have sat next to each other at one place).

Then—from [3]—the three men who sat next to each other could not have all sat on one of the longer sides of the table (the fourth man would have had to sit next to one of these men), and the middle man of the three men could not have sat on one of the shorter sides of the table. So the middle man of the three men must have sat on the end of a longer side.

From [1], [2], and [7], this middle man could not have sat in the victim's chair and the one man who sat between two women could not have sat in the chair opposite the victim (because in both of those cases the killer and the victim would not be of opposite sex, as required by [7]).

Then the arrangement of men and women around the table must have been one of the following ("M" stands for man and "W" stands for woman):

```
            M M W                           W M M
(a)   M              W        (b)   W              M
            W W M                           M W W
```

Then, from [4], [5], and [6], either:

```
      Husb  Nathan  Hostess        Hostess  Nathan  Husb
(a) Bro                  Wife  (b) Wife                  Bro
      Sister  Wife  Host              Host  Wife  Sister
```

From [1], [2], and [7], (a) is not the correct seating arrangement because the host's sister could not have been the victim. So (b) is the correct seating arrangement and the host was the victim; he was killed by his brother's wife. Thus, *Barbara was the killer.*

Deanna's Sister

Let

> P = number of Deanna's pennies
> N = number of Deanna's nickels
> Q = number of Deanna's quarters
> T = total cost of candy in cents
> a = number of Althea's candies
> b = number of Blythe's candies
> c = number of Carrie's candies
> d = cost of one gift in cents
> G = number of gifts

All the numbers involved are positive whole numbers.

From [1]: (1a) $P + N + Q = 13$ and (1b) $P + 5N + 25Q = T$
From [2] (2) $2a + 3b + 6c = T$
From [3]: (3) a, b, c are all different and all greater than 1
From [4] (4) $2a = 3b$, $2a = 6c$, or $3b = 6c$
From [5]: $G \times d = 480$
From [6]: $a + b + c = G$
From [7], the problem is "which is greatest: a, b, or c?"

There are six equations with nine unknowns, the fourth equation being one of three possibilities. There are too many equations to be able to use algebra alone in solving the problem; so additional characteristics of the numbers involved, besides the fact that they are all positive whole numbers, must be sought.

Now, the sum

of two odd numbers is always even,

of two even numbers is always even,

of one odd number and one even number is always odd.

Also, the product

of two odd numbers is always odd,

of two even numbers is always even,

of one odd number and one even number is always even.

From this information, in equation (1a) either all three of P, N, and Q are odd or only one of them is odd. T in equation (1b) is odd in either case (allowing each of P, N, and Q to be the only odd number in turn and allowing all three of P, N, and Q to be odd at the same time will establish this fact.) Then b in equation (2) is odd. Then, in (4), 2a cannot equal 3b because 2a is even and 3b is odd. Neither can 3b equal 6c because 6c is even and 3b is odd. So 2a = 6c. (At this point it is known that c is not the greatest because a has to be larger than c.) Dividing by 2, a = 3c. Substituting 3c for a in (6), b + 4c = G.

Now b is still odd; so, in b + 4c = G, G is odd. In (5), 480 is the product of two numbers, one of which is odd (G) and one of which is even (d). The only odd-number values possible for G in this product are 1, 3, 5, and 15. 1 and 3 are not possible values for G because b and c must both be positive whole numbers. 5 is not possible, from [3] (b and c cannot equal 1). So G must equal 15.

Then b + 4c = 15, and c cannot equal more than 3 or less than 1. From [3], c does not equal 1 or 3. So c must equal 2. Then b = 7. Because a = 3c from previous reasoning, a = 6. So b is greatest. Therefore, from [7], *Blythe is Deanna's sister.*

All other values can be found as follows. If G = 15, then—from [5]—d = 32. If a = 6, b = 7, and c = 2, then—from [2]—T = 45. Subtracting (1a) from (1b) gives 4N + 24Q = 32. Dividing by 4, N + 6Q = 8. Q is neither greater than 1 (otherwise N would be negative) nor less than 1 (there were three denominations, from [1]), so Q = 1. Then N = 2. Then, from (1a), P = 10.

The Cube

There are three possible arrangements of the figures on the faces of the cube, if the owner's statement is disregarded. Two of these arrangements are excluded by the owner's statement.

Either any one of the figures occurs only once on the cube or it occurs twice. If one figure is chosen, reasoning can then proceed. Which figure is it convenient to choose? Since both the ○ and the ● occur with four different figures, then—if one of them occurs only once—the figures on four other faces can be derived at once.

If the ● is chosen, then there are two possibilities, as previously mentioned: either ● occurs once or it occurs twice.

If the ● occurs once, then from the second view:

Then from the third view:

Finally, from the first view: either   or

I   II

If the ● occurs twice, then every other figure occurs only once.

From the second view:

The ○ pictured in the first view is the same ○ pictured in the second view.

So from the first view:

Then from the assumption that the ● occurs twice:

III

The third view checks out the assumption.

The figure on the bottom face in each view is recorded in the following table for each of the three possible arrangements. Also recorded is the figure that occurs twice in each arrangement.

111

	BOTTOM FIGURES			
	VIEW 1	VIEW 2	VIEW 3	REPEATED FIGURE
I.	●	■	⊕	○
II.	□	■	⊕	□
III.	●	■	⊕	●

From the owner's statement, arrangements II and III are not possible. So arrangement I is correct and *the ○ occurs twice.*

The Club Trick

From [7], four different suits were led.

At the club trick: from [2], everyone played a club.

At the diamond trick: from [4], diamonds were led first, so three diamonds were played; Deb must have been the only one not to follow suit and she must have played a spade (from [2], she followed suit at the club trick).

At the spade trick: only two spades were played (from [1] and [8]), so Bea must have played one of her hearts (from [2], she followed suit at the club trick and, from [4], she must have followed suit at the diamond trick); Cyd must have played a heart or a diamond (from [2], she followed suit at the club trick).

At the heart trick: Ada and Bea must have each played a heart (each was able to play one heart at this point, from previous reasoning); Deb must have played a spade (from [2], she followed suit at the club trick); and Cyd must have played a heart or a diamond (from [2], she followed suit at the club trick).

From previous reasoning and from [3], only two hearts were played at the heart trick. So Cyd played a diamond at the heart trick; then she must have played a heart at the spade trick.

The above conclusions concerning the suit played by each player at each trick are summarized in the following table:

	ADA	BEA	CYD	DEB
club trick	club	club	club	club
diamond trick	diamond	diamond	diamond	spade
heart trick	heart	heart	diamond	spade
spade trick	spade	heart	heart	spade

Diamonds were led first, from [4]. Clubs and hearts were not led second and third in either order because Cyd would not have been able to play a heart when spades were led (she must follow suit if she can). For the same reason, hearts were not led second.

Also, either the club trick followed the spade trick or the spade trick followed the club trick (from [1], Deb had only these two suits; from [5], she had to lead at one of these two tricks; from [8], she had to win the other of these two tricks).

Therefore, the order in which the suits were led was either:

      I. diamonds, spades, clubs, hearts

     II. diamonds, clubs, spades, hearts

From [5] and [6], the player who led the diamond won the heart trick. Only Ada and Bea played a heart at the heart trick; so this player is either Ada or Bea, from [8]. Then Ada or Bea led the diamond and the other of the two led the heart.

From [1] and [5], Deb must have led the spade (Ada and Bea led as previously indicated, and Cyd had no spades).

Therefore, *Cyd led the club.*

The analysis may be continued. Because the spade trick could have been won only by Ada (from [1], [5], [8], and the fact that Deb led the spade), clubs did not follow spades (because Cyd led the club and could not have won the spade). So order II must be the correct order. Then hearts followed spades and Ada led the heart. Then Bea led the diamond.

The play of the last four tricks is shown in the following table:

	ADA	BEA	CYD	DEB
diamond trick	followed suit	led	won	played a spade
club trick	followed suit	followed suit	led	won
spade trick	won	played a heart	played a heart	led
heart trick	led	won	played a diamond	played a spade

Twelve C's

$$\begin{array}{r} \overline{K} \\ C \\ \hline C \end{array}$$

$K + C = C$ implies $K = 0$.

A does not equal zero because $K = 0$ (or because the second partial product does not equal zero), and A does not equal 1 because the second partial product is not a duplicate of the first row (ABCDEFGH).

$$\begin{array}{r} \overline{E} \\ B \\ \hline C \end{array}$$

$K = 0$ implies E does not equal 0, which implies B is less than 9 (nothing was carried from $E + B$).

$$\begin{array}{r} A \\ \times \qquad A \\ \hline B \end{array}$$

B is less than 9 implies A is less than 3.

A does not equal 0 or 1 and A is less than 3 imply $A = 2$.

$A = 2$ and B is less than 9 imply $A \times B$ is less than or equal to 16.

$$\begin{array}{r} ABC \\ \times \qquad A \\ \hline B \end{array}$$

$A \times B$ is less than or equal to 16 implies that no more than 1 could have been carried to $A \times A$ ($A \times C$ cannot be more than 18, so no more than 2 could have been carried to $A \times B$).

So either $A \times A = B$ or $A \times A + 1 = B$. Then, because $A = 2$, either $B = 4$ or $B = 5$.

114

AB
×   J
—————
E

A = 2 implies J × A is less than or equal to 18; B = 4 or 5 implies J × B is less than or equal to 45. So E = 1 or E = 2.

Then, because A = 2, E = 1.

$$\begin{array}{c} \overline{E} \\ B \\ \hline C \end{array}$$

E = 1 and B = 4 or 5 imply C = 5, 6, or 7;

$$\begin{array}{c} A \\ \hline K \\ C \end{array}$$

while A = 2 implies C is even.

$$\begin{array}{c} \overline{GK} \\ EC \\ \hline C \end{array}$$

C = 5, 6, or 7 and C is even imply C = 6. Then G = 5.

Then B = 4.

$$\begin{array}{c} \overline{A} \\ F \\ \hline C \end{array}$$

Then F = 3.

$$\begin{array}{c} H \\ A \\ \hline \end{array}$$

Then H = 8.

$$\begin{array}{c} C \\ \hline \end{array}$$

$$\begin{array}{c} H \\ J \\ \hline C \end{array}$$

Then J = 7.

Then D = 9.

The multiplication is shown below:

```
      2 4 6 9 1 3 5 8
  ×               2 7
  ———————————————————
  1 7 2 8 3 9 5 0 6
  4 9 3 8 2 7 1 6
  ———————————————————
  6 6 6 6 6 6 6 6 6
```

115

John's Ideal Woman

From [1],

	BLUE-EYED?	SLENDER?	BLONDE?	TALL?
Ideal	yes	yes	yes	yes
1st Other	yes	yes		
2nd Other	yes	yes		
3rd Other				

Then, from [4],

	BLUE-EYED?	SLENDER?	BLONDE?	TALL?
Ideal	yes	yes	yes	yes
1st Other	yes	yes	no	
2nd Other	yes	yes	no	
3rd Other				

Then, from [2] followed by [4],

	BLUE-EYED?	SLENDER?	BLONDE?	TALL?
Ideal	yes	yes	yes	yes
1st Other	yes	yes	no	
2nd Other	yes	yes	no	
3rd Other	no		yes	yes

Then, from [7] followed by [3],

	BLUE-EYED?	SLENDER?	BLONDE?	TALL?
Ideal	yes	yes	yes	yes
1st Other	yes	yes	no	yes
2nd Other	yes	yes	no	no
3rd Other	no	no	yes	yes

NOTE: In the "TALL?" column, it makes no difference whether "no" is in the "1st Other" row or the "2nd Other" row.

116

From [6], there are four possibilities:

	(a)	(b)	(c)	(d)
Ideal	Betty	Carol		
1st Other			Betty	Carol
2nd Other			Carol	Betty
3rd Other	Carol	Betty		

From [8], (a) and (b) are not possible. There are again four possibilities:

	(c1)	(c2)	(d1)	(d2)
Ideal	Doris	Adele	Doris	Adele
1st Other	Betty	Betty	Carol	Carol
2nd Other	Carol	Carol	Betty	Betty
3rd Other	Adele	Doris	Adele	Doris

From [7], (c1) is not possible. From [5], (d1) is not possible.

Because (c2) and (d2) are the only remaining possibilities, *Adele is John's ideal woman*. Whether it is Betty or Carol that is not tall cannot be determined.

The L-Shaped Table

From [1] and [6] (using M for man, W for woman, Mh for host, and Wh for hostess), one of the following three arrangements is correct:

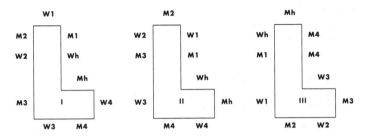

From [2] and [8], the host and the hostess and the two people sitting across from them are eliminated both as the killer and the victim in each arrangement; from [3] and [8], they are also eliminated as the spouses of the killer and the victim.

In each arrangement only one man and one woman sat across from each other. Therefore, from [2] and [3], the killer and the victim are of the same sex, and their spouses are of the same sex. So the man and the woman sitting across from each other are eliminated as both the killer and the victim in each arrangement; they are also eliminated as the spouses of the killer and the victim.

Therefore, the four key positions of killer, victim, killer's spouse, and victim's spouse—two pairs of married couples—must be contained in one of the following groups.

Grp. I: M1W1M2W3   Grp. II: M1W1M2W2M3M4
Grp. III: M1W2W3M4

Group I is impossible, from [4]. In Group II—from [4] and [5]—neither W1, W2, M1, nor M3 can be the killer or the victim; from [4], neither M2 nor M4 can be the killer or the victim. So Group II is impossible. Then Group III is the correct one. In Group III, from [4] and [5], neither M1 nor W2 can be the killer; from [7], W3 cannot be the killer. So M4 is the killer. Then *Ivan is the killer*. From [2], the victim is Cain.

The married couples turn out to be: Ivan (M4) and Fifi (W2), Cain (M1) and Hera (W3), Ezra (M2) and Joan (W4), and Gene (M3) and Dido (W1).

The Tenth Trick

From the fact that the four hands contained four cards in each suit and from [6], only one trump was played at each trick. So, from [2] through [5], each of three players did not have a suit that was led at some point, and one player led a trump at some point (because four different suits were led). Further, because a trump must have won each trick, the player who led the trump must have had two trumps and must have led a trump at the last trick, having won the next-to-last trick. (If he had won an earlier trick than next-to-last he would have remained with the lead and have led twice, contradicting [2] through [5], which require that four different players led.) Therefore, one player had two trumps, each of two other players had one trump, and one player had no trumps. From the distribution of the suits in the four hands, hearts or diamonds must be trump.

Counting the number of trumps in each of the players' hands is equivalent to counting the number of tricks won by each player. So, from [1] and [7], whether or not hearts or diamonds were trump, Hands I and II are two partners' hands and Hands III and IV are two partners' hands.

If diamonds were trump: Art held Hand III and led a diamond at trick thirteen, from [2]; Cab, from [7], held Hand IV and led a club at trick ten, from [4]. Because everyone had a club at this point, no one would have been able to play a trump at the club lead. So Cab did not lead at trick ten and, therefore, diamonds were not trump.

If hearts were trump (as they must have been), then by similar reasoning: Bob held Hand II and led a heart at trick thirteen, from [3]; Dan, from [7], held Hand I and led a spade at trick ten, from [5]. So either Art or Cab led at the eleventh trick, having won the tenth trick. Art could not have held Hand IV, from [2], so Cab held Hand IV and Art held Hand III. Then, Cab's hand held a spade at trick ten, while Art's hand held no spades. Thus, Art must have played a trump and *Art won the tenth trick.*

Below is the play of the remaining four tricks:

TRICK TEN—Dan led a spade, Art played a heart (trump) and won, Cab played a spade, and Bob played a club (or a diamond).

TRICK ELEVEN—Art led a diamond, Cab played a heart (trump) and won, Dan played a diamond, and Bob played a diamond (or a club).

TRICK TWELVE—Cab led a club, Bob played a heart (trump) and won, Dan played a club, and Art played a club.

TRICK THIRTEEN —Bob led a heart (trump) and won, Cab played a spade, Dan played a spade, and Art played a diamond.

Robert's Position

The points scored by the three men in the three events may be entered in a three-by-three square array as follows.

	POLE VAULT	LONG JUMP	HIGH JUMP
Robert			
Steven			
Thomas			

From [3a] and [3b], the totals of the scores in the columns and rows equal the same number. From [2] and [4], let the number of points scored by Robert and Thomas in the long jump be L points each. From [2] and [5], let the number of points scored by Robert and Steven in the high jump be H points each. From [1], [2], and [6], each of L and H may be 1, 2, or 3.

From [6], if Steven and Thomas both scored no points in the pole vault, then the array would look like this:

? L H   By comparing the first row with the first column, one can see
0 ? H   that it would be impossible for the total of Robert's three scores
0 L ?   to equal the total of the pole vault scores as required by [3a] and [3b].

Also from [6], if Steven scored no points in the long jump and Thomas scored no points in the high jump, then the array would look like this:

? L H   By comparing rows and columns one can see that, while L
? 0 H   could equal H, it would be impossible for Robert to score any
? L 0   points in the pole vault (as required) and satisfy [3a] and [3b] at the same time.

So either Steven scored no points in the pole vault and Thomas scored no points in the high jump, or Steven scored no points in the long jump and Thomas scored no points in the pole vault. Then either of these two arrays is possible:

ARRAY I.

? L H		? 1 2		1 1 2
0 ? H	So H = 2L*. So L = 1 and H = 2. Then	0 ? 2	Then	0 2 2
? L 0		? 1 0		3 1 0

*by comparing the second row with the second column

ARRAY II.

? L H		? 2 1		1 2 1
? 0 H	So L = 2H*. So H = 1 and L = 2. Then	? 0 1	Then	3 0 1
0 L ?		0 2 ?		0 2 2

*by comparing the third row with the third column

In either case, because one point is scored for third position, *Robert came in third in the pole vault.*

The Baseball Pennant

From [1], six games were played.

From [2] and the fact that six games were played, one team won three games, one team won two games, one team won one game, and one team won none of the games (there were no ties). Neither the Sexton team nor the Treble team could have won three games, from the fact that they each scored only one run (the lowest number scored) in a game. The Sexton team did not lose all three games because it scored the highest number of runs (7 runs) in one game. (S = Sexton team, T = Treble team, U = Ulster team, and V = Verdue team). So either:

    I. V won three games and T won no games,
   II. V won three games and U won no games,
  III. U won three games and T won no games, or
  IV. U won three games and V won no games.

The following reasoning uses [1], [3], and [4]:

If I is the correct situation, then T scored 6 to S's 7, then—from [4]—T scored 1 to V's 4, then T scored 4 to U's 6, then—from [4]—V scored 5 to U's 3, then V scored 2 to S's 1, and then S scored 3 to U's 2. Then these are the scores, arranged to represent rounds:

S T	T U	T V
7-6	4-6	1-4

V U	V S	S U
5-3	2-1	3-2

This situation contradicts [5], so it is eliminated.

If II is the correct situation, then U scored 6 to S's 7. Then U scored 2 to V's 5 or U scored 3 to T's 6. If the former, then U scored 3 to T's 4, but then V scored 4 to S's 3, which contradicts [3]. So U scored 3 to T's 6. Then U scored 2 to V's 4. Then either V scored 2 to T's 1, or V scored 2 to S's 1. If the former, then V scored 5 to S's 3. But then the last score would be S's 1 to T's 4, which contradicts [4]. So V scored 2 to S's 1. Then V scored 5 to T's 4, then S scored 3 to T's 1. Then, on the next page, these are the scores, arranged to represent rounds:

U S	U T	U V
6-7	3-6	2-4

V T	V S	S T
5-4	2-1	3-1

This situation contradicts [5], so it is eliminated.

If III is the correct situation, then T scored 6 to S's 7. Then T scored 1 against U or V. If U, then [4] could not be satisfied for the third game T played. So the other team was V, and V scored 4. Then T scored 4 to U's 6, then U scored 2 to S's 1, then U scored 3 to V's 2, then S scored 3 to V's 5. Then these are the scores, arranged to represent rounds:

T S	T V	T U
6-7	1-4	4-6

U V	U S	S V
3-2	2-1	3-5

This situation contradicts [5], so it is eliminated.

If IV is the correct situation, then —from [4] —V scored 4 to S's 7. Then V scored 5 to either U's 6 or T's 6. If V scored 5 to U's 6, then—from [4]—V scored 2 to T's 4. Then U scored 3 and 2 to S's 1 and T's 1 (in either order), so that S scored 3 to T's 6, contradicting [4]. So V scored 5 to T's 6 (not U's 6). Then V scored 2 to U's 3, then—from [4]—U scored 2 to S's 1, then—from [4]—U scored 6 to T's 4, then S scored 3 to T's 1. Then these are the scores, arranged to represent rounds:

V S	V U	V T
4-7	2-3	5-6

U T	S T	U S
6-4	3-1	2-1

This situation is the only one left and satisfies [5]. (The order of the first two rounds is immaterial.)

From [6], the V-T and U-S scores occurred during the last round. So the Alleycats are team V, the Cougars are team T, the Bobcats are team S, and the Domestics are team U.

Because situation IV is the correct one, U won all the games. Because U is the Domestics, *the Domestics won the pennant.*

No Cause for Celebration

There are four possible boy-girl combinations for the second and third children of each family ("s" stands for sister, "b" stands for brother):

second child	b	b	s	s
third child	b	s	b	s

From [1] and [2], these combinations can be developed as follows:

	I	II	III	IV
second child	b	b	s	s
third child	b	s	b	s
other children	b b s s	b b b s s	b b s	b b b s
totals	4b 2s	4b 3s	3b 2s	3b 3s

From [6] and the above combinations, one family has five children, one family has six children, and one family has seven children. Because only two families can have a sixth child, [5] indicates that the Smith family has five children; therefore, the Smith children are like those in combination III.

The following combinations are left for Brown and Jones:

	BROWN	JONES
(i)	4b-3s	4b-2s
(ii)	4b-3s	3b-3s
(iii)	4b-2s	4b-3s
(iv)	3b-3s	4b-3s

From [5], in (i) it is impossible for the number of brothers of one child in the Brown family to equal the number of sisters of one child in the Jones family.

Using the previous combinations for second and third children and referring to [3], [4] and [5], it is possible to begin expanding the combinations. It turns out that two variations are possible for each of (ii), (iii), and (iv).

	(II)			(III)			(IV)		
	BROWN 4B-3S	JONES 3B-3S	SMITH 3B-2S	BROWN 4B-2S	JONES 4B-3S	SMITH 3B-2S	BROWN 3B-3S	JONES 4B-3S	SMITH 3B-2S
1st									
2nd	b	s	s	b	b	s	s	b	s
3rd	s	s	b	b	s	b	s	s	b
4th		s	s		b	s		b	s
5th	s		b	b		b	s		b
6th	b	b		b	b		b	s	
7th									
1st									
2nd	b	s	s	b	b	s	s	b	s
3rd	s	s	b	b	s	b	s	s	b
4th		b	b		b	s		b	s
5th	s		b	s		s	s		b
6th	b	b		b	b		s	b	
7th									

The second tables for (iii) and (iv) are impossible from the total number of girls allowed for Smith and Brown, respectively.

The first table for (ii) is impossible from the total numbers of boys allowed for Jones and Smith and from [7].

The first table for (iv) is impossible from the total numbers of boys allowed for Brown and Smith and from [7].

In the second table for (ii), the seventh child of Brown must be a girl, from [8]. Then, from the totals for Brown, the first child must be a boy.

This firstborn has to be the only boy and this last born has to be the only girl, from [7] and [8] respectively. But these two children could not have married as required by [9]. So this table is impossible.

The only table left is the first table for (iii). Brown's column and Smith's column can be completed from the totals for Brown and Smith respectively. Then Jones' column can be completed from [7] and [8] and from the totals for Jones.

	BROWN 4b-2s	JONES 4b-3s	SMITH 3b-2s
1st	s	s	b
2nd	b	b	s
3rd	b	s	b
4th	s	b	s
5th	b	b	b
6th	b	b	–
7th	–	s	–

From [9], a Smith boy married a Jones girl. Therefore, *the Brown family had no cause for celebration that day*.

Index

WHAT IS MENSA?

Mensa
The High IQ Society

Mensa is the international society for people with a high IQ. We have more than 100,000 members in over 40 countries worldwide.

The society's aims are:

- to identify and foster human intelligence for the benefit of humanity;
- to encourage research in the nature, characteristics, and uses of intelligence;
- to provide a stimulating intellectual and social environment for its members.

Anyone with an IQ score in the top two percent of the population is eligible to become a member of Mensa—are you the "one in 50" we've been looking for?

Mensa membership offers an excellent range of benefits:

- Networking and social activities nationally and around the world;
- Special Interest Groups (hundreds of chances to pursue your hobbies and interests—from art to zoology!);
- Monthly International Journal, national magazines, and regional newsletters;
- Local meetings—from game challenges to food and drink;
- National and international weekend gatherings and conferences;
- Intellectually stimulating lectures and seminars;
- Access to the worldwide SIGHT network for travelers and hosts.

**For more information about
Mensa International:**
www.mensa.org
Mensa International
15 The Ivories
6–8 Northampton Street
Islington, London N1 2HY
United Kingdom

**For more information about
American Mensa:**
www.us.mensa.org
Telephone: 1-800-66MENSA
American Mensa Ltd.
1229 Corporate Drive West
Arlington, TX 76006-6103 USA

**For more information about
British Mensa (UK and Ireland):**
www.mensa.org.uk
Telephone: +44 (0) 1902 772771
E-mail: enquiries@mensa.org.uk
British Mensa Ltd.
St. John's House
St. John's Square
Wolverhampton WV2 4AH
United Kingdom

**For more information about
Australian Mensa:**
www.au.mensa.org
Telephone: +61 1902 260 594
E-mail: info@au.mensa.org
Australian Mensa Inc.
P.O. Box 212
Darlington WA 6070 Australia